Galton's Walk

T4-APU-667

Galton's Walk

Galton's Walk

Methods for the Analysis of
Thinking, Intelligence, and Creativity

Herbert F. Crovitz

Duke University

Harper & Row, Publishers
New York, Evanston, and London

GALTON'S WALK: *Methods for the Analysis of Thinking, Intelligence, and Creativity*
Copyright © 1970 by Herbert F. Crovitz

Printed in the United States of America. All rights reserved. No part of this book may be used or reproduced in any manner whatsoever without written permission except in the case of brief quotations embodied in critical articles and reviews. For information address Harper & Row, Publishers, Inc., 49 East 33rd Street, New York, N.Y. 10016

Library of Congress catalog card number: 72-108408

BF
455
.C75
1970

Dedication: To my family

10 - 13 - 70

Contents

Foreword

In these times of racial tension the name of Sir Francis Galton is likely to provoke more antipathy than respect from those who remember him only as the great proponent of eugenics. But Galton was a man of many parts. The man who argued so strongly that intelligence always follows the blood line, the author of *Hereditary Genius*, the man who first tried to develop mental tests as a basis for artificial selection in order to breed a race of supermen—this is not the Francis Galton who is honored in *Galton's Walk*.

It is not Galton the eugenicist, nor Galton the meteorologist, nor Galton the evolutionist, nor Galton the geographer, nor Galton the anthropologist, nor Galton the statistician who is commemorated in this little book. It is not even the Galton who wrote *The Art of Travel*, that fascinating handbook of advice for the nineteenth-century explorer, which explains how to arrange one's footwear most comfortably for extended walking.

Galton's Walk celebrates the Galton who invented the method of free association, and who first used it as he "walked leisurely along Pall Mall, a distance of 450 yards," taking careful note of all the thoughts associated with each object he saw. From that beginning Galton moved next to word associations, and concluded his observations with the remark that "our working stock of ideas is narrowly limited," and that "the mind continually recurs to them in conducting its operations."

The important word here is "recurs," for it was this idea that fired Herbert Crovitz's imagination. A basic, tractable fact of psychology, he points out, is the fact that everything recurs. It is well that it is so, for a world in which every experience was novel could hardly support intelligent life. From such basic facts, so obvious that they are easily overlooked, a scientist begins.

Where Crovitz goes from there is the story told in the following pages, so I will not spoil it by a *precis* here. It is an interesting story, and the reader who may become irritated by the frequent intrusion of the author's personal opinions is well advised to swallow his pique and move on. Like Galton, Crovitz is a psychologist both imaginative and practical, and the heuristics he develops are worthy of the most careful attention.

I think Sir Francis would have enjoyed it.

GEORGE A. MILLER

Preface

In 1879 Francis Galton, a friend and cousin of Charles Darwin, took a walk down Pall Mall in London. He was always walking somewhere, or traveling by other means, or writing books to assist travelers in distant climes. That particular walk, though, was in the interests of psychology, not geography. He took that walk to explore the structure of his mind; then he wrote an article about what he had discovered for the scientific journal, *Brain*.

That year, 1879, is always taken to be the year in which experimental psychology began, for in that year Wilhelm Wundt founded the world's first psychology laboratory. Wundt was a master of observation and generalization, while Galton was obsessed with finding practical uses for psychology. As E. G. Boring put it, "Wundt wanted to improve psychology; Galton, the human race."

Boring regretted that America overlooks Galton while it gives homage to Wundt, suspecting that Galton would not have been so remote to American psychologists if he had only come with Hermann von Helmholtz to the Chicago World's Fair of 1893. Of course, Helmholtz had cause to regret his trip, for on the return voyage he fell down the ship's staircase and died the next year—partly as a result of the injuries he had sustained.

In this book you will find Galton's 1879 article and its implications for thinking, intelligence, and creativity. These implications include an analysis of consciousness as an oscillating system, and a method for improving memory; an analysis of form versus content in language, and a method for turning difficult reading and writing into a simpler fill-in-the-blanks task; an analysis of the incompleteness of naturally occurring creativity, and a method for an active attack on creative problem-solving. These variations on a theme by Galton come from who I am—an experimental psychologist specializing in human binocular vision, and whose hobby is thinking about the structure of thinking.

I take this opportunity to name the four men I have learned the most from, though my thought never has the clarity of theirs. They are Gordon T. Gwinn, James N. Rees, Heinz Werner, and Karl Zener. I thank my son, Gordon Crovitz, for his help in measuring form versus content in the *Science* reports as they appear in Chapter 5. I also thank J. N. Rees, G. R. Lockhead, and Elaine K. Crovitz for their criticisms of the first draft of the manuscript. I was not able to follow all their wise suggestions. I must take full responsibility for all errors of omission and commission that remain.

HERBERT F. CROVITZ

Galton's Walk

1

Recurrence

My teacher, Stern, used to say that psychologists were
in the habit of putting obstacles in their path, and then
as they removed them one by one, calling attention
to the progress they were making.
HEINZ WERNER

Sciences begin with assuming ideal cases and observing tractable facts. It is somewhat oversimplified to say that physics began to make real progress when men took seriously the idea that on earth everything falls. Similarly, it is wrong to make too much of Lavoisier's beginning his reformation of chemistry with the single tractable fact that when a thing is heated it becomes larger. Nonetheless, present-day psychologists are sometimes asked to state a fact of their science with the generality of those from an early age of physics and chemistry. In psychological matters, the fact may be "everything recurs."

Study of the senses has led to many interesting and useful inventions, but the study of thought has been bloodless as stones. The fundamental fact of the sense of sight is that the eyes jump from place to place, but see only as the gaze pauses between jumps. Javal discovered those jumps late in the last century as he wondered how a child managed to read. He looked carefully at the eyes of a child reading, thus discovering "saccades," the discrete jumps the direction of gaze makes as the eyes move.

Thoughts jump like glances do. Just as we follow the outlines of an object with a glance made up of discrete jumps, we follow the contours of an idea with separable thoughts following each other in time. In looking around, we return to focusing upon some place in the visual field again and again. Since the number of possible fixation points is finite and comparatively small, we must go back to the same old fixation points again and again, whatever the stimulus may be. Similarly, the recurrence of thoughts must be common if the number of possible thoughts is similarly comparably small. In a lifetime of 70 years, with 16 hours of thought a day and an average of one thought a second, if no thought ever recurs, the number of a man's thoughts would exceed the product of $70(365)$ (16) (60) $(60) = 1,468,030,000$. In a single hour, by this estimate, 3,600 different thoughts would occur—unless thoughts take *more* than a second apiece, or unless they recur. I leave it to the reader to decide for himself whether there seem to be $16(3,600) = 57,000$ *different* second-long thoughts in his day. Since this issue cannot be decided at this time in any clear way, we proceed to the question of recurrence of thoughts from another point of view.

We suppose that we can, and do, have more than one thought on some topic, following along in time with thoughts on other topics intervening. Thoughts on some topics are never generated all at once, like close-packed peas falling from a pod that is soon forever emptied. What would a census of thoughts, arranged by topics and times, reveal? Such a census might reveal the demography of thought over time, much the way the census bureau charts the demography of population and the Public Health Service charts the demography of disease over time and space.

Long ago Galton inquired into the question of normative facial expression. Take a photograph of one member of some class of people and, without advancing the film, take an exposure of a second member of that group whose head is positioned in the same place, and continue through all the members of the group the same way. The result is a kind of composite group portrait in which common features are emphasized and unique ones lost. Just as features recur across people, thoughts recur across time. Ordinary group portraits keep the faces of members of the group separate. What is an analogous methodology for tracking thoughts that occur across time? The only method in wide use is to keep notes.

Analysis of the notebooks of artists or scientists, or other individuals who jot down their "ideas" would show that usually a person thinks consecutively on some topic over very long periods of time. Second, that in the temporal development of the "thoughts" of a person, successive unfoldings within a single direction are more common than switching the direction of thought.

There are many contents of consciousness that may seem stupid to jot down. They come and go, and their cycle of recurrence is unknown —except to the Germans of the nineteenth century, who noted everything and named it. Fechner noted the "haunting" of awareness by a recurring revival of a sensation consequent to an unusual intense stimulus and called it *Sinnesgedachniss*.

Sensory afterimages come and go, and as time marches they diminish and die. Just as they oscillate, so does recall. Memories pop into mind and out again, only to recur. Much can be made of cyclic events, and psychology has made something of this one, though it has tended to smother it with overconceptualization. To give one of the least mystifying examples Hull (1943) recognized the recurrence of memories and stuffed the phenomenon into the flaccid concept of the threshold, speaking of "oscillation at the threshold of recall." This is like saying that freezing rain is to be explained as "oscillation at the threshold of snow."

At the edge of plausibility, where advances in understanding are always made, oscillation of larger systems of things has emerged as a rather seductive problem. For example, von Békésy (1967), who has not forgotten his acoustical engineering, looks at the brain, with its feedback potentialities, and wonders why the whole thing does not go into oscillation.

A census of people over place and time always shows that some people are listed in successive listings, some of whom are listed in the same place over and over again; others are listed in one place, then another, then back, then forth—oscillating, say, from Bangor, Maine, to Miami, Florida. A full census of neural actions over time and place has not yet been made, any more than has a similar census of the raw contents of consciousness.

There are remarkable differences among people in the quality of their thought—not in how *well* they think, *qua* solve problems, but in the other sense of quality: the look, or the sound, or the smell, or the taste, or the touch of their consciousness. It has been called "imagery." Imagine a child's wooden block. Imagine that it is sawed in half, then each piece is sawed in half again. Of the remaining pieces, put one aside, but saw the rest in half. Now, assuming that you did not peek ahead, answer to yourself *not* how many pieces there are, which you are likely to have in mind, but rather: What was the *color* of the block and what did the sound of the sawing of the wood seem like? There are people with rather violent visual imagery who see the block all painted with designs and block letters, but do not hear the saw. There are people with strong auditory imagery who never notice the look of the block, but hear the rasp of saw on block. There are even people with strong "smell" imagery who notice the aroma of the sawdust. Well, the point should be made by now—people differ in their "imagery" just as people differ in the acuity of their various sense organs, even though the two may be entirely unrelated.

Were you to say you were near blind, you should be sent for spectacles; that you have no visual imagery, to the laboratory to invent metaspectacles. The problem would then be how you might proceed.

The first easy thing is to explore the limits. Later we will meet a Russian in the extreme of having visual and other imagery, Luria's mnemonist. It is worth noting now a pathetic case at the other extreme. He is a friend who is professionally interested in imagery, but was shocked when first reading Galton (1907) to find that such *odd* people exist. For himself, he claims that when he closes his eyes all is dark and he is gone. Silence and darkness and lack of stimulation deprive many of us of comfort, but they do not snuff "us" out. Yet, he insists that he is gone. But he dreams in visual images. Curious.

The second thing to explore is an analogy. Consider the difference between vision and visual imagery, as things that can be hampered or improved. Well, eyes come with various degrees of excellence with respect to how well one sees with them. But no matter how they come, the technology for changing your visual acuity is well developed. Put lenses of various types between your eye and a scene, and your view of the scene will change accordingly—as if by magic, but "really" by geometrical optics. Furthermore, given an eye that spectacles can make to see, a single constant *miraculous* device will on nearly any eye restore what vision fancy lenses would. The device is an artificial pupil, merely a pinhole in a card.

The theory that relates to why now the blur is gone is that now only the light coming straight through the center of your lens is left in the game, and sources of dislocation of the light "rays" are left out. That is the reason the "image" is sharp; the reason it is dim is that only the fraction of the light that comes that path is effective, and brightness depends on *amount*. The source of blur in vision is the scatter of the light "rays" caused by defective lenses and associated parts of the eye— for those cases that spectacles, or pinholes, will relieve. The job that either optical device does is to rectify the scatter of the light that would happen naturally in bad eyes. In extreme cases of scatter, nothing but a rather pretty blur is seen without optical devices. Optometry fits spectacles that remove the blur that replaces sharp vision; let us designate a putative future discipline, analogous but interested in imagery, as *cognometry*. At some other time, when this problem comes to be solved by some future founder of cognometry, one will perhaps be fitted with metaspectacles that remove the blur that replaces sharp imagery. To generalize from the packed ironies surrounding discoveries in the history of science, you now have the analog to pinhole spectacles at hand, but do not know it.

Similarly, we probably could order a cognoscope from off the shelf of some laboratory supply house where it is sold under some other name for some other purpose. A cognoscope, another thing to invent, is a putative device analogous to the ophthalmoscope invented by Helmholtz (1962). The ophthalmoscope consists of a flashlight and a half-silvered mirror. The flashlight is to send light into an eye; the half-silvered mirror is to allow the doctor to see into the eye without his head getting into the way.

What would a cognoscope do? Well, the ophthalmoscope exhibits distortions in the path of light. Perhaps a cognoscope would exhibit distortions in the path of a thought. It is the *relations* among thoughts over *time* that counts, as in sensory matters like visual acuity it is the relations among light over *space* that counts, as we shall soon see.

Naive, as well as oversophisticated, psychology takes "the self" very seriously. It was David Hume who denied that "the self" is more than a made-up fancy. He said that it is not perceived.

For my part, when I enter most intimately into what I call *myself*, I always stumble on some particular perception or other, of heat or cold, light or shade, love or hatred, pain or pleasure. I never catch *myself* at any time without a perception, and never can observe anything but the perception . . . (and though there are some who assert they do perceive their selves) . . . I may venture to affirm of the rest of mankind that they are nothing but a bundle or a collection of different perceptions, which succeed each other with inconceivable rapidity, and are in a perpetual flux and movement (Hume, 1739).

There is no harm in holding on to "the self"—but tuck it into a corner, for now we begin. Let us take the last part of the quote from Hume with cold-blooded seriousness. About that part there can be no holding back. We are a bundle of perceptions. They succeed each other at some rate equivalent for Hume to inconceivable rapidity, and there is some variety, a perpetual flux and movement. The variety, the flux, and the movement reduce to what he already said: that there is a bundle of perceptions, one after the other at some rate—something like inconceivable rapidity.

Numerous writers have held that the contents of consciousness change over time. Ernst Mach (1959, p. 250) even supposed that the period of time that is felt to pass is measured by the number of contents that pass in that time, noting that time seems long when "attention is severely forced" but short during easy employment. He went even further, guessing at a discovery still not convincingly made, that to find the organic consumption connected to consciousness one should find the organic consumption that varies, as does time sensation.

Yet we had better recognize some choices concerning the change in the contents of consciousness over time. We might assume that thoughts occur in single steps, that one follows another and each uses up some time. Were it not single-step, more than one could happen at a given time.

Thoughts are either gummed together in a muddy rapids, or in a clear rapids down which they plunge separately. The decision here is easy—it is impossible to describe and distinguish thoughts without labeling them. In order to proceed, we must suppose quantized thoughts, individual ones, shooting Hume's rapids.

But do they come along in single steps? There is a widely held theory, namely Freud's, that supposes there are three minds: a conscious one, a preconscious one, and an unconscious one, all grumbling and grousing and gadding about together. Take a slice through this sandwich at time t and you will find, presumably, three thoughts—one in the conscious layer, one in the preconscious layer, and one in the unconscious layer. Contrast this three-layer theory to an n-layer theory that would say that there are as many thoughts active at time t as you like. But one lonely one sits a moment atop the mound. In either the three-layer theory or the n-layer theory, one thought at a time is open to inspection, if any are at all: the one on top, the one we *have* at a given moment. Should we be so fortunate as to accept the idea that there exists a thought at time t that is open for inspection, we had better grab it, leaving the other layers out of the game.

We now begin to pry into Hume's bundle. First, we ask a question that can be asked of any bundle whatever, namely, *Is the bundle a plenum?* A plenum is defined as an aggregation with no empty spaces. Most bundles seem to have empty spaces. But the bag that is the Universe is fully packed. According to Descartes, it is fully packed with matter; according to Leibnitz and Einstein, it is fully packed with relations. Modern physicists do not believe in empty space, as Russell noted in his analysis of the abstract and the historical features of the plenum issue (Russell, 1945, pp. 68–71). Where there is no matter, there are electromagnetic waves, say, but matter itself is just one label for grouping events, and light waves is just another. "It is events that are the *stuff* of the world, and each of them is of brief duration."

In earlier times, Heraclitus was on one side of the fence with Parmenides on the other. Heraclitus emphasized the changes of things over time. Parmenides emphasized the lack of empty spaces. In olden times, everyone agreed that these views are incompatible, for how can there be movement in a plenum? As Russell points out, all shared this mistake. In a bundle that is not a plenum, things can move about by moving into empty spaces, a thing shoving into a space in a complex, apparently haphazard, way. But in a plenum, a bundle with no empty spaces, there can only be one kind of movement: a *cyclic* movement. What a lovely simplification!

Pack into a loose bag the cars of a toy railroad, and shake them up. There is very complex movement of the cars—nonplenum movement. But take the cars out and put them on the track, tightly packed, each car butting against the next, even unto the back of the last car up against the front of the first car.

Now we are on the track! The trains go round and round. Engine—coal car—oil car—passenger car—mail car—caboose—engine—coal car—oil car—passenger car—mail car—caboose—engine—coal car—oil car—passenger car, etc. We now enlarge on the simplification which asserts that thought is a plenum—close-packed thoughts going round and round in a groovy track.

We do not greet birds that fly too fast to see and sing too high to hear. To inspect fast-moving machines whose parts have some regular rate of recycling, we use a stroboscope. This instrument flashes a light at some adjustable, regular rate. When the flash rate is right, we can see a stopped image of the fast-moving cyclic event. For rather slow-moving repetitive events, it is fun to toy with using the eyelids to simulate a stroboscope—keeping them closed, then popping them open, then keeping them closed, then popping them open, then keeping them closed, etc. In this way the tempo of glimpses out at the environment simulates the mechanism of a stroboscope.

Imagine a universe in which visual perception—the whole set of events associated with the arrival of light at the retinal surface—is incompatible with thought, the inspection of events in "the mind's eye." Suppose that events in the mind's eye cycled, so that every few seconds a particular thought recurred, but the rate of change in the mind's eye was very large, so that in a fraction of a second that thought is gone, only to be cycling on its track to reappear in a few seconds. To get a stopped image of a thought in the mind's eye, creatures in that universe might blink their eyes at some rate.

In our universe, the blinking of eyes is a great mystery, as the facts that are known up until now indicate. The lion blinks less than once a minute; some monkeys blink at an average of 45 times a minute. Blind people have normal blink rates. Humidity does not affect blink rate. In the blink, the upper lid closes like a window shade upon the lower lid. Blinks occur during sleep. The average interblink interval among adult men is 2.8 seconds; in adult women, 4.0 seconds. The duration of a full blink is between 300 and 400 milliseconds (Adler, 1965; Davson, 1963).

The eyeblink is part of the startle response, in which all becomes tense and alert. The eyeblink is associated with cognitive effort—during mental multiplication, say, the eyeblink rate may go to 50 blinks a minute.

Given a blink that lasts 300 milliseconds every 3 seconds, there are about 20,000 blinks a day, with about 1¾ hours spent in eyeblinks in the average waking day. Similarly, about 1¾ hours a night are spent in dreaming. Would one dream less if one blinked more? Are eyeblinks microsleep, as Sartre supposed in *No Exit?*

In truth, are perception and cognition incompatible at time *t?* Kahneman, Beatty and Pollack (1967) had subjects monitor a visual signal, trying to keep track of its changing contents, while engaged in a mental arithmetic task. Mental exercise sets the eyes to blinking, and it also sets the pupil of the eyes to swelling. Eye-watchers now conclude that the pupil dilates and constricts as muscle tension and/or thought waxes and wanes. From use of moment-to-moment changes in pupil size, as related to work on the arithmetic and probability of detection of the visual signal, the authors concluded that there is some degree of functional blindness while one is engaged in thought.

To track the size of the pupil from afar by photography, and to take its size as a mark of thought, is rather technical and rather indirect. Scientists frequently choose such ways. When Galton in Africa marveled at the physical proportions of native girls, he would have rather used a tape measure, but he did not know the language and chose not to ask missionaries to be translators for this project. But measure he must:

I sat at a distance with my sextant, and as the ladies turned themselves about, as women always do, to be admired, I surveyed them in every possible way and subsequently measured the distance of the spot where they stood—worked out and tabulated the results at my leisure. I have been measuring other things all the time I have been here, for I have been working hard to make a good map of the country (Pearson, 1914, Vol. 1, p. 232).

Take a normal case, good eyes and all the rest, a willing heart, a clear head, and a steady unchanging stimulus, a 1,000-Hz pure tone at 40 db. Let the investigator of this situation be Georg von Békésy, the best investigator of these matters alive as this is being written. In his retrospective book, Békésy (1967) reports that, as the unvarying tone goes on, perception of the tone changes about once a second; its apparent loudness momentarily decreases. But then it returns to its prior level of apparent loudness—continuing to oscillate to moments of "a certain momentary lack of consciousness." Its period, as he reports, is from 0.8 to 1.2 seconds.

I do not know if the experiment has been made tracking the cycle of fading of *two* simultaneous discriminable tones, say, but it does not seem very likely that *everything* goes out like a candle every now and then.

Yet to suppose it might on the fast track measured in fractions of a second is, a priori, no more whimsical than to recognize that it does on the slow track measured in fractions of a day. It is no more dotty to assume that eyeblinks are micronaps than to speculate that sleep is a rather long blink. Surely, during sleep, we admit that there is a certain lack of consciousness with respect to outside stimuli.

You may be reminded of rocking a baby to sleep, with a repetitive rhythmic rocking. In my experience, the rocking need not at all be rhythmic when the infant is very young, for at that time, the first month or two of life, any sort of motion seems to put them to sleep, much as if they were creatures subject to the freezing of animal hypnotism. This may be the case even before the baby is born. When the mother moves about, the fetus tends to be quiet in the womb; it is when she lies down and her motion stops that the fetus begins to thrash about, as if it has been awakened by the quiet.

Periodic response of a system to unchanging input is the rule down to the level of analysis of the single neuron. Lillie (1929) immersed an iron wire with a thin oxide coating into a nitric acid bath. With one end of the wire in the acid, waves of surface depolarization travel along the wire; in the wake of each such wave the coating is formed anew. Lord Adrian (1932) chose Lillie's iron-wire model to investigate the problem of the phasic response of single neurons to steady stimulation, and this is still appropriate.

How long can a content of consciousness be held in "the mind's eye" absolutely unchanging? After what interval does it change? I have heard of Eastern masters who can, in meditation, hold a thought without change for hours; but as for myself, the interval is on the order of a fraction of a second. I picture to myself the Eiffel tower, but soon the flag topping it begins to wave, a taxi toots its horn on the road below, and a boulevardier raps his stick on the curb. I greatly enjoy the play of images, but I despise their import, for they wave, and toot, and rap to tell me that David Hume was right—the perceptions that make up consciousness succeed one another with inconceivable rapidity.

We fall back on a similar moment in the history of the study of the action of the nervous system, and it may restore our confidence. The story is pretty well known, and it refreshes the spirit. Once upon a time there was Hermann von Helmholtz, a boy sent to medical school by the government on condition that upon graduation he serve a hitch as an army doctor. And so he did, but Helmholtz was one who seized the day—at Berlin where he was stationed was a grand university at which he made his way into the groups surrounding Magnus in physics and Müller in physiology. From the encounter with Magnus came Helmholtz's famous paper on the conservation of energy. From his encounter with Müller, came Müller's annoying assertion that the speed of conduction along a nerve is of inconceivable rapidity—its speed was to be considered as about the same as the speed of light. When Helmholtz left Berlin to take his first teaching job, he took a shot at measuring the speed of neural conduction and found that it was somewhat variable, but on the order of 200 miles per hour.

You might take yourself to a quiet comfortable place and, after sitting a half-hour in the dark to get rid of lingering afterimages, and assuming you are still awake, you might picture to yourself the Eiffel tower, and see how long until it changes—*it* being the whole of consciousness, *or*, if you like, just the content of the mind's eye, leaving the mind's ear, nose, throat, etc., out of the game.

Or you might prefer a different attack on the problem; a measure of how fast perceptions in the mind's eye *can* cycle.

In the very simple case of an analog to the cff, a measure of the speed the mind can cycle can be made. The cff refers simply to the number of times per second a light can go on and off until it starts to look steadily on, rather than flickering. We can try to think of a flickering light in the mind's eye. We can think of it (if we have "visual imagery") as going on and off slowly, or more and more quickly. We can, between successive periods of imagining its flickering, look at a stroboscope that *is* flickering at some physically measured rate. At some rate the strobe's flicker becomes "fused"—separate flickers cannot be discriminated. At this rate, on the order of 50 Hz, we have reached the cff. Perhaps we can cycle the light past 50 Hz in "the mind's eye," perhaps 500 Hz, perhaps 5,000 Hz. To find out the fact of this matter, an experiment has been done. There is a rate beyond which an imaginary flicker cannot be made faster without losing the discriminability of successive imaged on-periods. That rate is on the order of 5 Hz.

The analogous thing can be done for auditory cycling by having a real versus an imaginary tick-tick-tick-tick in which the rate of auditory flutter turning into steadiness can be compared in sensation and imagination, given subjects with auditory imagery. Well, again, the limit in sensation is on the order of 50 Hz, whereas in imagination it is on the order of 5 Hz.

Hume can be counted, and Hobbes may have exaggerated a bit when he described a rather long train of ideas as happening in a moment of time, "for thought is quick." On the average, is thought so quick?

No, for the wheels of mental life in imagination are by an order of magnitude slower than the wheels of the mental life in the perception consequent to the rush of stimuli outside.

Given that sensation can change as thought cannot, still *thought surpasses action*. It takes longer to run down the stairs than one can imagine that act, even though one can see someone run faster than one can imagine it and hear his footfalls faster than one can call them to mind, clip-clop. There is one simple possibility that, were it true, would make this state of affairs a matter of no great surprise—namely, if these differences tapped differences in the underlying inertia (resistance to change). The *physical system that must move over distances* in the case of real running is large; there is lots of inertia in that physical system. In seeing someone run, much less physical inertia—just the rather trifling amounts associated with photoreception and recoding into neural events, then spark-jump-spark-jump-spark-jump, etc., as electric charges pop along neurons and jump across synapses. In thought, there is some intermediate amount of inertia. *What is moving that intermediate amount?*

I do not know. But I do know about the motor theory of thought that points to the little bits of tensing that do go on in the appropriate muscles as one thinks of doing something (Max, 1934). That seems a candidate for a medium inertia system, but the issue is entirely open.

"Time travels in divers paces with divers persons. I'll tell you who time ambles withal, who time trots withal, who time gallops withal, and who he stands still withal."

Shakespeare assigned time's horses to particular people at particular interesting times of life. We might assign time's horses another way and say this of time: It ambles with action, trots with thought, gallops with sensation, and stands still for the eventual descendent of Galton who, armed with Fourier analysis and a census of the cycles of recurrence, will adjust his protostrobe to catch us in stopped motion.

2
Recurrence and consciousness

In all scientific procedure we begin by marking out a
certain region or subject as the field of investigation; to this
we must confine our attention leaving the rest of the
universe out of account till we have completed the
investigation in which we are engaged.
JAMES CLERK MAXWELL, 1877

In a distinction made by Polya (1957, p. 154), there are two sorts of problems: "problems to find" and "problems to prove." The "problem to find" has the aim of coming up with a certain object or action. "We may try to find, to obtain, to acquire, to produce, or to construct all imaginable kinds of objects." In the mystery story, the murderer. In a chess problem, the move. In riddles, a word. In elementary algebra, a number. In geometry construction problems, a figure.

On the other hand, in a "problem to prove" the aim is to come up with a conclusive answer to the question "true or false?" We have to prove something. If we seek to prove that the sum of any two angles of a triangle equals two right angles minus the third angle, the problem as it is given, without transforming it, calls out for use of the set of geometric operations. Nonetheless, it is always possible to take a shot at transforming a lovely mathematical problem into the bulky form of mechanical models or into the messy form of words. Sometimes when this is done the tables can be turned cleverly; for example, to replace the usual technique of using mathematics to produce solutions to problems in mechanics, by using mechanics to produce solutions to problems in mathematics. An elegant move in that upsetting direction was made by the very distinguished statistician Uspenskii (1961). His book shows a variety of mathematical problems that, when transformed into mechanical analogs, can be "solved" easily.

We must take the problems associated with transformation very seriously, for we do not know the content of the plenum that we postulate. But we do know *some* requirements for any plenum. The requirements are: (1) there are a number of contents and (2) the contents form a series that recycles at some rate.

Where in the world is an analogous system? Suppose that we first

13

decide to label the contents, to distinguish one from the next. Now we cycle the labels. How has it ever been done, this cycling of labels? How can we recycle a list of names, or of prepositions, or anything we want to remember or recite?

Hastings *et al.* (1928) describe rosary beads and prayer wheels. A rosary is "a string of knots or beads, designed as an aid to the memory." Using a system of knots as mnemonic signs was widespread, from the *quipu* system of keeping records of Peru in which meaning was signaled by the particular kind of knot of particular colored cord to the similar sign-system of knots used in China in the time of Yung-ching-che.

The oldest reference to rosaries in the literature of India is said to be in the Jain canon, where they are said to be one of the devices of Brahmanical monks. The encyclopedia quotes from the Buddhist "forty-two points of doctrine." Rosaries made of beads vary in number in the forms available in the beginnings of our century. The number tends to be 108 beads, the number of mental conditions of the Buddhist texts, and 108 also is the number of beads for a votary of Vishnu. A worshiper of Siva is said to use a rosary of 32 or 64 beads. By the thirteenth century, the making of rosary beads, called "paternosters," was a specialized industry in Paris and London. The Buddhists of the North had a different design than a string of knots or beads. They had, in recorded history, wheels or cylinders made to revolve for a run through whatever was inscribed. "Gabriel Bonvalot mentions having encountered in the monastery of Doton, 100 large bobbins, each containing 10,000 invocations. As a few minutes suffice to revolve the whole in succession, one may thus rapidly gain the benefit of the indulgences attached to the recitation of 1,000,000 formulas" (Hastings *et al.*, 1928, vol. 10, p. 213). The simple device is just a wheel or a cylinder, attached to a wooden handle, with an eccentric weight, so a flick of the wrist gets and keeps the thing revolving as one repeats, "Oh, the jewel in the lotus."

In the present context, this appears to be mixing up two ways to run through a list. The wheel could give the labels in some order, as, of course, could rosary beads with the labels on separate beads, or fashioned into separate labeled knots. But so does the sentence of the form "the jewel *in* the lotus." There you have *jewel* and *lotus* and *in*. Where did the *other* sentences go?

To have other sentences to chant calls for an entirely oral tradition, separate from fingering through the labels to *see* them, instead reciting a poem to allow you to *hear* them.

One might consider laboring in the shade of Robert Graves' (1958) *White Goddess*, in which he sought to read the riddle of the ancient Câd Goddeu in which that scholarly poet argued that the ancient poems referred to names of trees. But was he misguided, unable to see the forest for the trees? That is, was there a poetic tradition of running through some words, that like other such traditions—prayer wheels, strings of beads—became a victim of ossification? Consider a poem of this form:

I was the blade *of* a sword
Believe me *when* it appears
I was a raindrop *in* the air
I was light *from* the sky
I was a book *after*
I was a bridge for passing *over*
Forty-two rivers.
I journey *as* an eagle
I am a boat *on* the sea
I am enchanted *for* a year
I fight *though* I am small
Before the ruler of Britain,
Around his fleets . . . (etc.)

If you remembered it was the little words and *not* the rest, such a poem would be a portable mnemonic for prepositions, to carry around in your memory. A much different form from any of these mnemonics may underlie the *I Ching*, a book of ancient Chinese magic that is based upon a very elegant pattern. There are 64 patterns that sticks may fall into when put in an 8 by 8 matrix, as the *I Ching* seems to do. It also could be used as the same old run through the possibilities. It seems to be so orderly a puzzle that many have agreed with Mohl, quoted in the Dover edition (Legge, 1963): "I like it, for I come to it out of a sea of mist, and find solid ground"—though the design of a plenum to be consistently and exhaustively displayed by tossing to earth a pile of sticks seems hard.

One might think about what it would be like to explicitly run through the list of labels by using one of the devices described above, and what it would be like to use the list for an aid to memory. Spinning out the set of labels is in vain, for a machine could do it while you were doing something that was more fun, like playing with the devices themselves. Or if the mood is serious, not frivolous, by turning the devices to serious ends—such as religious ones—that those devices have existed for. The wish for the sheer bare frivolity of playing with the devices, or in more serious moods, the wish for perfectibility of emotions through meditating on the devices for higher ends, may strip the devices of their possible usefulness as mnemonics. Indeed, given the evanescence of empire and the shiftings of time, well accepted by all before the modern idea of progress over time took the fancy of almost all, frivolity (one emotion) and religious feeling (another emotion) may last longer than anything else. In the extreme case, the devices described herein may be the ossified descendents of a prehistoric civilization that once had them as a mnemonic, but fell before our history began. It is an interesting fancy. Were that civilization to be just like ours is now, what could it have done to help the next cycle of civilization? Knowing the mnemonic devices on which civilization could be rebuilt would perhaps ossify and come to naught—Where would we put what sign for the next cycle, to grin at them when they eventually again come to where we now are? I leave the puzzle stated, but without a solution. I would tell you if I knew.

The opposite possibility is there too; namely, that indeed there is a Deity who seeded this planet with those devices for use in prayer. Omniscience might recognize that, when the devices became ossified for sacred uses, they would be available for secular uses. The issue cannot be determined by me.

But certainly devices like prayer wheels or rosary beads are formally similar to our plenum—labeled contents that cycle, one after another. What we have done is to take a prayer wheel as a model of consciousness.

The history of psychological theory is a struggle between champions of two opposed analogies. One has had it that some psychological matter is like some physical system. The other has had it that some psychological matter is like some mental-content. An example of the former case is the Young-Helmholtz theory of color vision, in which it is held that color mixing done by the organism's body and/or mind is like the color mixture done as a child spins a varied-colored top. The opposing example is the Hering theory of color vision that holds that the organism's body and/or mind is organized in accordance with opponent-processes, just as complementary colors are opposite in conscious experience. There is no great mysterious force in this duality of analogy, for it is essentially exhaustive. Physical systems concern matter, and conscious experience concerns mind. Having taken analogies to mind and to matter, not much is left except for a Pythagorean fascination with number, and eschatological matters which may be best left waiting in the wings—perhaps where the action is, but presumably hidden from scientific examination.

Traditionally, treatments of any hard intellectual topic either begin with a statement of the difficulty of defining the important terms to be developed, or end with the conclusion that truly meaningful definition of the terms that have been used will be the main task of future generations. Sometimes both infirmities are displayed the moment pen is put on paper. Hans-Lucas Teuber (1960) begins his excellent chapter on perception with the statement that it may be strange to find a chapter on perception in a handbook of neurophysiology, especially since there is no adequate definition of perception and no neurophysiological theory. The problem of definition of terms and of statement of theory is like the problem of writing a menu. It is rather easy to say what it is one thinks he has eaten, rather more difficult to decide what to order, and most difficult to write the menu before the groceries have been delivered from the market, especially if one orders from a whimsical grocer who seldom delivers what you order. In many cases in science, one cannot know beforehand what will be found out, or even what will be interesting at a better-informed tomorrow. How can we *use* the plenum *today?*

Our treatment of the concept of a plenum as the form of thought is a very "mechanical" one. Of course, opinions still differ. One man says that there is a mind and there is a body, one spiritual and the other material with the immaterial mind never affecting the material body. Another man says that there is a soul that carries around a corpse, that the immaterial mind is the controller of the material body. Another man says that consciousness may be as material as chicken soup, the task remains to *find* it.

When Descartes understood animals to be like machines, he began a dreamy tradition of impious cant from which we may recover when a chimpanzee joins the army and a man loses to a dolphin at a game of Twenty Questions. Even today a chimpanzee is earning her way to an interesting life by slowly learning the American sign-language usually taught to deaf mutes (Gardner and Gardner, 1969). Whether a machine like a digital computer with arms could do it even faster was a question that was not in Descartes' game. For when he came out for animal automatism, he had his physiologist's hat snugly on his head.

Descartes did anatomy; he cut animals apart and spread the word that animals are mere machines, or automata, devoid of both reason and consciousness. After all, he argued, every movement that an animal makes is made through physical movement of parts of its body, and even in man complex behavior can occur without any thought whatsoever upon that action. There is no proof but that animals merely simulate intelligence when they do intelligent-appearing things —or, we could add, simulate idiocy when they do stupid-appearing things. But it is all a simulation done by a senseless hulk. T. H. Huxley reviewed the work of Descartes in this matter and pushed the analysis one step further. Men, he said, are automata too, but conscious ones. "It seems to me," he wrote, "that in men, as in brutes, there is no proof that any state of consciousness is the cause of change in the motion of the matter of the organism . . . the feeling we call volition is not the cause of a voluntary act, but the symbol of that state of the brain which is the immediate cause of that act." Huxley made his views all the more clear:

I protest that if some great Power would agree to always make me think what is true and do what is right, on condition of being turned into a sort of clock and wound up every morning before I got out of bed, I should instantly close with the offer. The only freedom I care about is the freedom to do right; the freedom to do wrong I am ready to part with on the cheapest terms to any one who will take it off me (Huxley, 1895, pp. 192–193).

On these matters both Descartes and Huxley argued quite cleverly, but Huxley gave the game away by supposing that, after all, free will was possible for brutes and men. Automaton theory has never stopped short of descriptive analyses of consciousness—it is just that material-its disagree with the common assumption that consciousness is the *cause* of anything else (Gray, 1968). Descartes supposed that there were involuntary acts and voluntary acts, the former running off without conscious control, but the latter depending on it. This distinction even has anatomic and neurophysiological support of a rather weak kind: There are some motor pathways that act *after* a wish. But the best word was had by Douglas Spalding (1874), who likened the opinion that voluntary movements take their rise in feeling and are guided by intellect to the belief that the movements of a locomotive take their rise in noise and are guided by smoke. Looking back today at that past, to say that animals are like machines seems to be a pedestrian image, though at an earlier time it may have seemed different. Nonetheless, Ernst Mach (1959) did well to overstep the easy comparison of animals to machines; he wrote:

the best physical image of a living process is still afforded by a conflagration, or some similar process, which automatically transfers itself to the environment. A conflagration keeps itself going, produces its own combustion-temperature, brings neighboring bodies up to that temperature and thereby drags them into the process, assimilates and grows, expands and propagates itself.

And then to cap it off, "Nay, animal life itself is nothing but combustion in complicated circumstances."

The issue of the relevance of consciousness to behavior is still alive, and it becomes heated when one considers men who are suffering from having a spinal cord severed from the brain, and men with a left cerebral hemisphere that is severed from the right cerebral hemisphere. Even Huxley knew about the first case, though Descartes did not. In general, the symptomatology of spinal man consists of reflexes that are disconnected from cleverness. That which the spinal cord can do, it does. By Huxley's day, it was known that spinal-cord reflexes can be pretty complex, but cleverness was left out when spinal cords were designed. More recent discoveries made by Sperry show that cleverness was not put into right cerebral hemispheres, either. Consider a few cases of an odd disorder—the severing of the corpus collosum, neural links at a high level that connect the left and the right cerebral cortex. Give such a patient an apple, some keys, a ring, and some cotton, one by one, and have him name them with his eyes closed and letting him touch them only with one hand—the left hand, which connects with the right brain, and the right hand, which connects with the left brain. The left hand gets a key; the patient says, "Oh, that's the apple," or gets the cotton and calls it a ring. It is all a randomness. If the class of objects is remembered, it's the connection between the words and the feeling of the objects that is ruined. Yet, put the objects in the right hand, and there is no problem at all. Everything is named correctly. The way this tends always these days to be thought of is that words live in the left hemisphere. In the severed case, the left-hand feelings that are at work in the right hemisphere cannot make contact with the words, but the patient guesses. The right hemisphere is rather a dumbbell, the spinal cord is rather stupid too, and where oh where in the left hemisphere does all the cleverness reside? Well, in Broca's area, my beamish boy—wordy language lives. Does language make all the difference?

To what extent is *action* mindless? How would a man behave on a day his consciousness was away? Assuming that everything else was tuned up, he would be absent-minded. But put the toothbrush into his hand, have the car keys in their usual pocket, put dinner before him, and the day would probably seem rather dull but commonplace. For much of a day is put to habits that run off without a mind tending to them—and the question now is: What difference, if any, does the presence of that mind make? Spend the day with an image of a metronome in your head pushing out all else, as compared to a day when you are "with it," entirely. What distinguishes those days? It is not that on the second you do more new things, for you can easily stumble into things of freshness in a state of absent-mindedness, though you may not recognize it.

But absent-mindedness is not quite the same as empty-headedness, for when the mind is on something else it is on *something*; a tattered end of a discarded thought may be just what the hand needs to do some unnoticed practical thing.

In physics, "causal laws" are so implausible and complex that one can get nowhere in trying to infer them from the perception of obvious things, but we do lazily suppose that cause does stand bare before us in psychology. I want to pinch my ear, and lo, I do it! The whole conception of cause comes cheaply out of volition, the temporal bond between ideas to do easy things and the rather quick doing of them.

Indeed, there is an intention before many an act, and action sometimes follows intent. But what goes on in thought and in nerves and in muscles in the time that intervenes between the wish and the pinch? Further, what had preceded the conscious wish? When the time comes that we want to do some simple thing, we sometimes do it soon. That ability does give a rather breezy impression of free will and the determination of one's destiny.

Lest you think all is determined to make you just like everyone else by some Fate that seeks uniformity, there is a rather convincing silly experiment you can do right now. Get a pair of dice, or some other way to generate random numbers between 2 and 12. Turn chance to use. Very likely, when you think of pinching your ear you do so. Consider these alternatives:

2. Pinch your ear
3. Pinch your nose
4. Pinch your cheek
5. Pinch your thigh
6. Pinch your arm
7. Clap your hands
8. Slap your knees
9. Pucker up your lips
10. Stick out your tongue
11. Smile broadly
12. Pull your ear

Now roll your pair of dice, or check the position of the second hand of your watch, or in some other way let chance select one of the numbers. Having gotten a number, go ahead and do the action described. Most likely, you rolled a seven, if you used dice which have a pro-seven bias through the laws of probability, given how the numbers on each of the dice can combine, and dice rollers in this experiment mostly clap their hands. But however you get your number, get numbers a dozen times and do your dozen things in order. Now you may rest content that you are unique, that you did a sequence no one else would ever have done, for chance gives too big a domain for you to meet another like you now. This little experiment on a miniature case of free will means that the gods allow variety; and if you are a clockwork orange, at time t you are like none other and whenever random rippling through a set of conceivable alternatives can enter in, you hold uniqueness and creativity in your grasp.

By such lights a machine with some *randomness* built in is *creative* too. I do not fear that turn of events, for I think that creativity is small potatoes indeed, and this book presents a case for that view of the matter.

Let the set of allowable actions be greater than the 2 to 12 in this little experiment, and let you have a way to pick them randomly, and do the ones you can, after selecting the ones you like. Why, surprise, surprise! That describes man at his freest. Of course, the trouble is that you do not know the set of *all* possible actions and you do not have a reliable way to go through the set of them either *fully or randomly*. That's why you keep doing all the old dull things, over and over again.

The anti-hero of Anthony Burgess' *A Clockwork Orange* (1962) was being dragged away to therapy that would henceforth restrict him to doing only what was right. "How about me?" he yelled, "Am I just to be like a clockwork orange?" T. H. Huxley would have been delighted to be in that condition, but times have turned and none of us would. We seek irreverent dreams now.

3

Recurrence and memory

In modern psychology, great discoveries are made daily,
only to be shrouded in ad hoc theories, prescientific
and semimetaphysical.
L. S. VYGOTSKY

Bertrand Russell was once asked to contribute to a book on how to think clearly. He answered the editor with a regretful letter saying he could be no help, for thinking in him was instinctive as digestion—he fills up with relevant information; goes about his business thinking of other things; later, with time and good fortune, he notices that the work is done. Less urbane views of the matter have been put forward: principally the view that there is an unconscious mind in which the work is done according to some rules concerning the random pairing of ideas, like collisions on a jiggly plenum.

The pairing of ideas can be of varying quality, and superordinate post hoc considerations have always been brought into these matters. For instance, Ernst Jones (1956) gave the opinion that T. H. Huxley missed genius for he was all scepticism and no credulity.

On the other hand, Galton was not one whit sceptical, that great gull of creation. He could go along and lose his way, finding that he was taking a walk on the wild side. Such was his walk along Pall Mall, published in 1879 (Galton, 1879). Here is recurrence discovered and made a little bit clear.

Karl Pearson, when the Galton Professor at the University of London (Pearson, 1914), commented with faint bitterness that while Galton had broken new ground here, nobody among English psychologists had carried the work forward. Pearson supposed the reason might be that it is easier to experiment with another person's mind than with one's own.

The paper starts on the next page. It is reprinted from *Brain*, July 1879, with permission of the publisher.

PSYCHOMETRIC EXPERIMENTS
By Francis Galton, F.R.S.

Psychometry, it is hardly necessary to say, means the art of imposing measurement and number upon operations of the mind, as in the practice of determining the reaction-time of different persons. I propose in this memoir to give a new instance of psychometry, and a few of its results. They may not be of any very great novelty or importance, but they are at least definite, and admit of verification; therefore I trust it requires no apology for offering them to the readers of this Journal, who will be prepared to agree in the view, that until the phenomena of any branch of knowledge have been subjected to measurement and number, it cannot assume the status and dignity of a science.

The processes of thought fall into two main categories: in the first of these, ideas present themselves by association either with some object newly perceived by the senses or with previous ideas; in the second process, such of the associated ideas are fixed and vivified by the attention, as happen to be germane to the topic on which the mind is set. In this memoir I do not deal with the second process at all, so I need not speak more in detail concerning it, but I address myself wholly to the first. It is an automatic one; the ideas arise of their own accord, and we cannot, except in indirect and imperfect ways, compel them to come.

My object is to show how the whole of these associated ideas, though they are for the most part exceedingly fleeting and obscure, and barely cross the threshold of our consciousness, may be seized, dragged into daylight, and recorded. I shall then treat the records of some experiments statistically, and will make out what I can from them.

I should be glad if the reader would refer to an article written by me in the 'Nineteenth Century' of last March, which was based on the observations I am about to describe. It travels somewhat further afield than the present memoir, but does not enter so much into details.

When we attempt to trace the first steps in each operation of our minds, we are usually baulked by the difficulty of keeping watch, without embarrassing the freedom of its action. The difficulty is much more than the common and well-known one of attending to two things at once. It is especially due to the fact that the elementary operations of the mind are exceedingly faint and evanescent, and that it requires the utmost painstaking to watch them properly. It would seem impossible to give the required attention to the processes of thought and yet to think as freely as if the mind had been in no way preoccupied. The peculiarity of the experiments I am about to describe is that I have succeeded in evading this difficulty. My method consists in allowing the mind to play freely for a very brief period, until a couple or so of ideas have passed through it, and then, while the traces or echoes of those ideas are still lingering in the brain, to turn the attention upon them with a sudden and complete awakening; to arrest, to scrutinise them, and to record their exact appearance. Afterwards I collate the records at leisure, and discuss them and draw conclusions. It must be understood that the second of the two ideas was never derived from the first, but always directly from the original object. This was ensured by absolutely withstanding all temptation to reverie. I do not mean that the first idea was of necessity a simple elementary thought: sometimes it was a glance down a familiar line of associations, sometimes it was a well-remembered mental attitude or mode of feeling, but I mean that it was never so far indulged in as to displace the object that had suggested it, from being the primary topic of attention.

I must add, that I found the experiments to be extremely trying and irksome, and that it required much resolution to go through with them, using the scrupulous care they demanded. Nevertheless, the results well repaid the trouble. They gave me an interesting and unexpected view of the number of the operations of the mind, and of the obscure depths in which they took place, of which I had been little conscious before. The general impression they have left upon me is like that which many of us have experienced when the basement of our house happens to be under thorough sanitary repairs, and we realise for the first time the complex system of drains and gas- and water-pipes, flues, bell-wires, and so forth, upon which our comfort depends, but which are usually hidden out of sight, and of whose existence, so long as they acted well, we had never troubled ourselves.

The first experiments I made were imperfect, but sufficient to inspire me with keen interest in the matter, and suggested the form of procedure that I have already partly described. My first experiments were these. On several occasions, but notably on one when I felt myself unusually capable of the kind of effort required, I walked leisurely along Pall Mall, a distance of 450 yards, during which time I scrutinised with attention every successive object that caught my eyes, and I allowed my attention to rest on it until one or two thoughts had arisen through direct association with that object; then I took very brief mental note of them, and passed on to the next object. I never allowed my mind to ramble. The number of objects viewed was, I think, about 300, for I have subsequently repeated the same walk under similar conditions, and endeavouring to estimate their number, with that result. It was impossible for me to recal in other than the vaguest way the numerous ideas that had passed through my mind;

but of this, at least, I was sure, that samples of my whole life had passed before me, that many bygone incidents, which I never suspected to have formed part of my stock of thoughts, had been glanced at as objects too familiar to awaken the attention. I saw at once that the brain was vastly more active than I had previously believed it to be, and I was perfectly amazed at the unexpected width of the field of its everyday operations. After an interval of some days, during which I kept my mind from dwelling on my first experiences, in order that it might retain as much freshness as possible for a second experiment, I repeated the walk, and was struck just as much as before by the variety of the ideas that presented themselves, and the number of events to which they referred, about which I had never consciously occupied myself of late years. But my admiration at the activity of the mind was seriously diminished by another observation which I then made, namely that there had been a very great deal of repetition of thought. The actors in my mental stage were indeed very numerous, but by no means so numerous as I had imagined. They now seemed to be something like the actors in theatres where large processions are represented, who march off one side of the stage, and, going round by the back, come on again at the other. I accordingly cast about for means of laying hold of these fleeting thoughts, and, submitting them to statistical analysis, to find out more about their tendency to repetition and other matters, and the method I finally adopted was the one already mentioned. I selected a list of suitable words and wrote them on different small sheets of paper. Taking care to dismiss them from my thoughts when not engaged upon them, and allowing some days to elapse before I began to use them, I laid one of these sheets with all due precautions under a book, but not wholly covered by it, so that when I leant forward I could see one of the words, being previously quite ignorant of what the word would be. Also I held a small chronograph, which I started by pressing a spring the moment the word caught my eye, and which stopped of itself the instant I released the spring; and this I did so soon as about a couple of ideas in direct association with the word had arisen in my mind. I found that I could not manage to recollect more than two ideas with the needed precision, at least not in a general way; but sometimes several ideas occurred so nearly together that I was able to record three or even four of them, while sometimes I only managed one. The second ideas were, as I have already said, never derived from the first, but always direct from the word itself, for I kept my attention firmly fixed on the word, and the associated ideas were seen only by a half glance. When the two ideas had occurred, I stopped the chronograph and wrote them down, and the time they occupied. I soon got into the way of doing all this in a very methodical and automatic manner, keeping the mind perfectly calm and neutral, but intent and, as it were, at full cock and on hair trigger, before displaying the word. There was no disturbance occasioned by thinking of the imminent revulsion of the mind when the chronograph was stopped. My feeling before stopping it was simply that I had delayed long enough, and this in no way interfered with the free action of the mind. I found no trouble in ensuring the complete fairness of the experiment, by using a number of little precautions, hardly necessary to describe, that practice quickly suggested, but it was a most repugnant and laborious work, and it was only by strong self-control that I went through my schedule according to programme. The list of words that I finally secured was 75 in number, though I began with more. I went through them on four separate occasions, under very different circumstances, in England and abroad, and at intervals of about a month. In no case were the associations governed to any degree worth recording, by remembering what had occurred to me on previous occasions, for I found that the process itself had great influence in discharging the memory of what it had just been engaged in, and I of course took care between the experiments never to let my thoughts revert to the words. The results seem to me to be as trustworthy as any other statistical series that has been collected with equal care.

On throwing these results into a common statistical hotchpot, I first examined into the rate at which these associated ideas were formed. It took a total time of 660 seconds to form the 505 ideas; that is at about the rate of 50 in a minute or 3000 in an hour. This would be miserably slow work in reverie, or wherever the thought follows the lead of each association that successively presents itself. In the present case, much time was lost in mentally taking the word in, owing to the quiet unobtrusive way in which I found it necessary to bring it into view, so as not to distract the thoughts. Moreover, a substantive standing by itself is usually the equivalent of too abstract an idea for us to conceive it properly without delay. Thus it is very difficult to get a quick conception of the word "carriage," because there are so many different kinds—two-wheeled, four-wheeled, open and closed, and all of them in so many different possible positions, that the minds possibly hesitates amid an obscure sense of many alternatives that cannot blend together. But limit the idea to, say, a landau, and the mental association declares itself more quickly. Say a landau coming down the street to opposite the door, and an image of many blended landaus that have done so, forms itself without the least hesitation.

Next, I found that my list of 75 words gone over 4 times, had given rise to 505 ideas and 13 cases of puzzle, in which nothing sufficiently definite to note occurred within the brief maximum period of about 4 seconds, that I allowed myself to any single trial. Of these 505, only 289 were different. The precise proportions in which the 505 were distributed in quadruplets, triplets, doublets or singles, is shown in the uppermost lines of Table 1. The same facts are given under another form in the lower lines of the table, which show how the 289 different ideas were distributed in cases of fourfold, treble, double, or single occurrences.

1

Recurrent associations
(FROM GALTON, 1879)

Total number of associations		Occurring in			
		Quadruplets	Triplets	Doublets	Singles
No.	505	116	108	114	167
%	100	23	21	23	33

Total number of different associations		Occurring			
		Four times	Three times	Twice	Once
No.	289	29	36	57	167
%	100	10	12	20	58

I was fully prepared to find much iteration in my ideas, but had little expected that out of every hundred words twenty-three would give rise to exactly the same association in every one of the four trials; twenty-one, to the same association in three out of the four, and so on, the experiments having been purposely conducted under very different conditions of time and local circumstances. This shows much less variety in the mental stock of ideas than I had expected, and makes us feel that the roadways of our minds are worn into very deep ruts. I conclude from the proved number of faint and barely conscious thoughts, and from the proved iteration of them, that the mind is perpetually travelling over familiar ways without our memory retaining any impression of its excursions. Its footsteps are so light and fleeting, that it is only by such experiments as I have described that we can learn anything about them. It is apparently always engaged in mumbling over its old stores, and if any one of these is wholly neglected for a while, it is apt to be forgotten, perhaps irrecoverably. It is by no means keen interest and attention when first observing an object, that fixes it in the recollection. We pore over the pages of a "Bradshaw," and study the trains for some particular journey with the greatest interest; but the event passes by, and the hours and other facts which we once so eagerly considered become absolutely forgotten. So in games of whist, and in a large number of similar instances. As I understand it, the subject must have a continued living interest in order to retain an abiding-place in the memory. The mind must refer to it frequently, but whether it does so consciously or unconsciously, is not perhaps a matter of much importance. Otherwise, as a general rule, the recollection sinks, and appears to be utterly drowned in the waters of Lethe.

The instances, according to my personal experience, are very rare, and even those are not very satisfactory, in which some event recalls a memory that had lain *absolutely* dormant for many years. In this very series of experiments, a recollection which I had thought had entirely lapsed appeared under no less than three different aspects on different occasions. It was this: when I was a boy, my father, who was anxious that I should learn something of physical science, which was then never taught at school, arranged with the owner of a large chemist's shop to let me dabble at chemistry for a few days in his laboratory. I had not thought of this fact, so far as I was aware, for many years; but in scrutinising the fleeting associations called up by the various words, I traced two mental visual images (an alembic and a particular arrangement of tables and light), and one mental sense of smell (chlorine gas) to that very laboratory. I recognised that these images appeared familiar to me, but I had not thought of their origin. No doubt if some strange conjunction of circumstances had suddenly recalled those three associations at the same time, with perhaps two or three other collateral matters which may still be living in my memory, but which I do not as yet identify, a mental perception of startling vividness would be the result, and I should have falsely imagined that it had supernaturally, as it were, started into life from an entire oblivion extending over many years. Probably many persons would have registered such a case as evidence that things once perceived can never wholly vanish from the recollection, but that in the hour of death, or under some excitement, every event of a past life may reappear. To this view I entirely dissent. Forgetfulness appears absolute in the vast majority of cases, and our supposed recollections of a past life are, I believe, no more than that of a large number of episodes in it, to be reckoned in hundreds or thousands, certainly not in tens of hundreds of thousands, which have escaped oblivion. Every one of the fleeting, half-conscious thoughts which were the subject of my experiments admitted of being vivified by keen attention, or by some appropriate association; but I strongly suspect that ideas which have long since ceased to fleet through the brain, owing to the absence of current associations to call them up, disappears wholly. A comparison of old memories with a newly-met friend of one's boyhood, about the events we then witnessed together, shows how much we had each of us forgotten. Our recollections do not tally. Actors and incidents that seem to have been of primary importance in those events to the one, have been utterly forgotten by the other. The recollection of our earlier years are, in truth, very scanty, as any one will find who tries to enumerate them.

My associated ideas were for the most part due to my own unshared experiences, and the list of them would necessarily differ widely from that which another person would draw up who might repeat my experiments. Therefore one sees clearly, and I may say, one can see *measurably*, how impossible it is in a general way for two grown-up persons to lay their minds side by side together in perfect accord. The same sentence cannot produce precisely the same effect on both, and the first quick impressions that any given word in it may convey, will differ widely in the two minds.

I took pains to determine as far as feasible the dates of my life at which each of the associated ideas was first attached to the word. There were 124 cases in which identification was satisfactory, and they were distributed as in Table 2.

2

Relative number of associations formed at different periods of life
(FROM GALTON, 1879)

Total number of different associations		Occurring								Whose first formation was in
		Four times		Three times		Twice		Once		
No.	%	No.	%	No.	%	No.	%	No.	%	
48	39	12	10	11	9	9	7	16	13	Boyhood and youth
57	46	10	8	8	7	6	5	33	26	Subsequent manhood
19	15	—	—	4	3	1	1	14	11	Quite recent events
Totals:										
124	100	22	18	23	19	16	13	63	50	

It will be seen from the table that out of the 48 earliest associations no less than 12, or one quarter of them occurred in each of the four trials; of the 57 associations first formed in manhood, 10, or about one-sixth of them had a similar recurrence, but as to the 19 other associations first formed in quite recent times, not one of them occurred in the whole of the four trials. Hence we may see the greater fixity of the earlier associations, and might measurably determine the decrease of fixity as the date of their first formation becomes less remote.

The largeness of the number 33 in the fourth column, which disconcerts the run of the series, is wholly due to a visual memory of places seen in manhood. I will not speak about this now, as I shall have to refer to it further on. Neglecting, for the moment, this unique class of occurrences, it will be seen that one-half of the associations date from the period of life before leaving college; and it may easily be imagined that many of these refer to common events in an English education. Nay further, on looking through the list of all the associations it was easy to see how they are pervaded by purely English ideas, and especially such as are prevalent in that stratum of English society in which I was born and bred, and have subsequently lived. In illustration of this, I may mention an anecdote of a matter which greatly impressed me at the time. I was staying in a country house with a very pleasant party of young and old, including persons whose education and versatility were certainly not below the social average. One evening we played at a round game, which consisted in each of us drawing as absurd a scrawl as he or she could, representing some historical event; the pictures were then shuffled and passed successively from hand to hand, every one writing down independently their interpretation of the picture, as to what the historical event was that the artist intended to depict by the scrawl. I was astonished as the sameness of our ideas. Cases like Canute and the waves, the Babes in the Tower, and the like, were drawn by two and even three persons at the same time, quite independently of one another, showing how narrowly we are bound by the fetters of our early education. If the figures in the above table may be accepted as fairly correct for the world generally, it shows, still in a measurable degree, the large effect of early education in fixing our associations. It will of course be understood that I make no absurd profession of being able by these very few experiments to lay down statistical constants of universal application, but that my principal object is to show that a large class of mental phenomena, that have hitherto been too vague to lay hold of, admit of being caught by the firm grip of genuine statistical inquiry.

The results that I have thus far given are hotch-potch results. It is necessary to sort the materials somewhat, before saying more about them.

After several trials, I found that the associated ideas admitted of being divided into three main groups. First there is the imagined sound of words, as in verbal quotations or names of persons. This was frequently a mere parrot-like memory which acted instantaneously and in a meaningless way, just as a machine might act. In the next group there was every other kind of sense-imagery; the chime of imagined bells, the shiver of remembered cold, the scent of some particular locality, and, much more frequently than all the rest put together, visual imagery. The last of the three groups contains what I will venture, for want of a better name, to call 'histrionic' representations. It includes those cases where I either act a part in imagination, or see in imagination a part acted, or most commonly by far, where I am both spectator and all the actors at once, in an imaginary mental theatre. Thus I feel a nascent sense of some muscular action while I simultaneously witness a puppet of my brain—a part of myself—perform that action, and I assume a mental attitude appropriate to the occasion. This, in my case, is a very frequent way of generalising, indeed I rarely feely that I have secure hold of a general idea until I have translated it somehow into this form. Thus the word 'abasement' presented itself to me, in one of my experiments, by my mentally placing myself in a pantomimic attitude of humiliation with half-closed eyes, bowed back, and uplifted palms, while at the same time I was aware of myself as of a mental puppet, in that position. This same word will serve to illustrate the other groups also. It so happened in connection with 'abasement' that the word 'David' or 'King David' occurred to me on one occasion in each of three out of the four trials; also that an accidental misreading, or perhaps the merely punning association of the words 'a basement,' brought up on all four occasions the image of the foundations of a house that the builders had begun upon.

So much for the character of the association; next as to that of the words. I found, after the experiments were over, that the words were divisible into three distinct groups. The first contained 'abbey,' 'aborigines,' 'abyss,' and others that admitted of being presented under some mental image. The second group contained 'abasement,' 'abhorrence,' 'ablution,' &c., which admitted excellently of histrionic representation. The third group contained the more abstract words, such as 'afternoon,' 'ability,' 'abnormal,' which were variously and imperfectly dealt with by my mind. I give the results in the upper part of Table 3, and, in order to save trouble, I have reduced them to percentages in the lower lines of the table.

We see from this that the associations of the 'abbey' series are nearly half of them in sense imagery, and these were almost always visual. The names of persons also more frequently occurred in this series than in any other. It will be recollected that in Table 2 I drew attention to the exceptionally large number, 33, in the last column. It was perhaps 20 in excess of what would have been expected from the general run of the other figures. This

3

*Comparison between the quality of the words and that of the ideas
in immediate association with them*
(FROM GALTON, 1879)

Number of words in each series		Sense imagery	Histrionic	Purely verbal		Total
				Names of persons	Phrases and quotations	
26	'Abbey' series	46	12	32	17	107
20	'Abasement' series	25	26	11	17	79
29	'Afternoon' series	23	27	16	38	104
75						290
	'Abbey' series	43	11	30	16	100
	'Abasement' series	32	33	13	22	100
	'Afternoon' series	22	25	16	37	100

was wholly due to visual imagery of scenes with which I was first acquainted
after reaching manhood, and shows, I think, that the scenes of childhood
and youth, though vividly impressed on the memory, are by no means
numerous, and may be quite thrown into the background by the abund-
ance of after experiences; but this, as we have seen, is not the case with
the other forms of association. Verbal memories of old date, such as Biblical
scraps, family expressions, bits of poetry, and the like, are very numerous,
and rise to the thoughts so quickly, whenever anything suggests them, that
they commonly outstrip all competitors. Associations connected with the
'abasement' series are strongly characterised by histrionic ideas, and by
sense-imagery, which to a great degree merges into a histrionic character.
Thus the word 'abhorrence' suggested to me, on three out of the four
trials, an image of the attitude of Martha in the famous picture of the
raising of Lazarus by Sebastian del Piombo in the National Gallery. She
stands with averted head, doubly sheltering her face by her hands from
even a sidelong view of the opened grave. Now I could not be sure how
far I saw the picture as such, in my mental view, or how far I had thrown
my own personality into the picture and was acting it as actors might act
a mystery play, by the puppets of my own brain, that were parts of myself.

As a matter of fact, I entered it under the heading of sense-imagery, but it might very properly have gone to swell the number of the histrionic entries.

The 'afternoon' series suggested a great preponderance of mere catchwords, showing how slowly I was able to realise the meaning of abstractions; the phrases intruded themselves before the thoughts became defined. It occassionally occurred that I puzzled wholly over a word, and made no entry at all; in thirteen cases either this happened, or else after one idea had occurred the second was too confused and obscure to admit of record, and mention of it had to be omitted in the foregoing table. These entries have forcibly shown to me the great imperfection in my generalising powers; and I am sure that most persons would find the same if they made similar trials. Nothing is a surer sign of high intellectual capacity than in the power of quickly seizing and easily manipulating ideas of a very abstract nature. Commonly we grasp them very imperfectly, and hold on to their skirts with great difficulty.

In comparing the order in which the ideas presented themselves, I find that a decided precedence is assumed by the Histrionic ideas, wherever they occur; that Verbal associations occur first and with great quickness on many occasions, but on the whole that they are only a little more likely to occur first than second; and that Imagery is decidedly more likely to be the second, than the first, of the associations called up by a word. In short, gesture-language appeals the most quickly to our feelings.

It would be very instructive to print the actual records at length, made by many experimenters, if the records could be clubbed together and thrown into a statistical form; but it would be too absurd to print one's own singly. They lay bare the foundations of a man's thoughts with curious distinctness, and exhibit his mental anatomy with more vividness and truth than he would probably care to publish to the world.

It remains to summarise what has been said in the foregoing memoir. I have desired to show how whole strata of mental operations that have lapsed out of ordinary consciousness, admit of being dragged into light, recorded and treated statistically, and how the obscurity that attends the initial steps of our thoughts can thus be pierced and dissipated. I then showed measurably the rate at which associations sprung up, their character, the date of their first formation, their tendency to recurrence, and their relative precedence. Also I gave an instance showing how the phenomenon of a long-forgotten scene, suddenly starting into consciousness, admitted in many cases of being explained. Perhaps the strongest of the impressions left by these experiments regards the multifariousness of the work done by the mind in a state of half-unconsciousness, and the valid reason they afford for believing in the existence of still deeper strata of mental operations, sunk wholly below the level of consciousness, which may account for such mental phenomena as cannot otherwise be explained. We gain an insight by these exepriments into the marvellous number and nimbleness of our mental associations, and we also learn that they are very far indeed from being infinite in their variety. We find that our working stock of ideas is narrowly limited, but that the mind continually recurs to them in conducting its operations, therefore its tracks necessarily become more defined and its flexibility diminished as age advances.

Galton's recognition of recurrence was marvelous. But the experiment was terrible! Poor Galton would believe almost anything that allowed measurement and maintained an air of mystery.

Galton concluded the stock of the mind's store was sparse from the recurrence of "associations" to the same stimulus:

I had fully expected to find much iteration in my ideas, but had little expected that out of every hundred words, twenty-three would give rise to exactly the same association in every one of the four trials; twenty-one to the same association in three out of the four, and so on, the experiments having been purposely conducted under very different conditions of time and local circumstances.

How could Galton then, or we today, be sure that the responses to those recurrent stimuli were "associations" rather than "memories"? Surely they were *not* independent trials, for the subject was purposely the same one. Give me the stimulus "abhorrence" and let me then picture to myself a dramatic cartoon showing poor Martha looking on as Lazarus is made to rise from the dead; and if it is *vivid* enough, the next time the stimulus is "abhorrence" the response is quite likely to be poor Martha, and along with her a memory that this all happened the same way before. The important feature of that work is that, indeed, it points to the way to tie stimuli to responses, to make memory near to perfect, to *always* make the same association. The way, of course, is to attach responses to stimuli with vividness. It is the sparsity of vivid images that is important; the methodical assignment of them is the method of mnemonists.

This shows much less variety in the mental stock of ideas than I had expected, and makes us feel that the roadways of our minds are worn into very deep ruts. I conclude from the proved number of faint and barely conscious thoughts, and from the proved iteration of them, that the mind is perpetually travelling over familiar ways without our memory retaining any impression of its excursions. Its footsteps are so light and fleeting that it is only by such experiments as I have described that we can learn anything about them. It is apparently always engaged in mumbling over its old stores . . .

Galton, thus, described recurrence and only just missed formalizing the mind as an oscillatory system and discovering a very practical use for a walk down Pall Mall. The use is well known to mnemonists. *One learns a map, then places images to be remembered at locations along it.* Actually one does not need to remember a map if you have one drawn out.

Luria wrote a book about a mnemonist who had a spectacular memory, and convinced people he had a very concrete and childlike synesthetic approach to the world, going as far as commenting that Vygotsky had a crumbly, yellow voice (Luria, 1968, p. 24). The study of the mnemonist by Luria and his associates at Moscow University covered 30 years. It began when the mnemonist came to Luria's laboratory to have his memory tested, for the mnemonist, who was then a newspaper reporter, annoyed his editor by not forgetting assignments while not taking notes like everyone else had to do. Luria treats the facts of the matter with a great deal of wonderment and awe. The mnemonist could be given a list of words or numbers and repeat it back in any order at some years after it was first given him. His one major complaint, at an early stage of his career, was that he could not forget.

Nancy Waugh (1968) did reply to that book with commendable balance, noting that the mnemonist, as described, merely had a lively habit of transforming abstract things into lively images, and along with that transformation, an assimilation of the images into a recoverable coherent scheme—quick thinking rather than a photographic memory.

The concretization of abstract matters is a widespread dimension on which people tend to vary spontaneously. Duncker (1945, p. 111) noted that the distinguishing characteristic between "good" and "poor" mathematicians is the habit that the latter have of transforming matters into concrete images, that "many people" make their thought material precise and stable by restructuring it into "perceptual structurings."

This is very good for mnemonists and poets, but not so good for mathematicians. And as bad as it is for mathematicians, an analysis of the locus of the evil has yet to be made. Duncker (1945) studied this mathematical problem: "Why are all six-digit numbers, of the form 267,267;* 591,591; 112,112; divisible by 13?" Soon we will be attuned to the profound rumblings of taking two of the same thing, and then we are likely to go right to the center of it—immediately asking how to make the same group of three digits before and after a comma. Well, we say, the comma just refers to the thousands place. Multiply three digits by a thousand and you get the three digits followed by a comma and three zeros. Multiply the three digits by 1,001, and you get the three digits followed by a comma and the same three digits. A sign of progress, we say perhaps; for every number of the form *abc,abc* is just *abc* times 1,001, and so conversely any number of the form *abc,abc* is divisible by 1,001. Then, if 1,001 were divisible by 13, all numbers of the form *abc,abc* would also be divisible by 13. We do the division, finding that indeed 1,001 divided by 13 comes out even— the quotient is 77. So! How lovely is mathematics! We have come upon another problem to smile at; for now we can ask the uninitiated this problem: Why are all numbers of the form 267,267; 591,591; 112,112 divisible by 77? This seems even more devilish than Duncker's 13 problem, for its form is so *wrongly* suggestive.

In describing the contents of his consciousness as he set about remembering a long list of things, Luria's mnemonist would picture in his mind's eye a street that he already *did* remember well. He then pictured to himself a mental walk along the street—frequently Gorky Street in Moscow—and imagined putting "images" at locations along the street.

Transforming material to be remembered into images, and attaching the images to locations on an accessible map, allowed the recall of a great deal of information, in any sequence required—for sequence had become transformed into location on the mental map of that street.

As Luria pointed out (p. 33), other mnemonists also have used the technique of beginning with a stable well-learned mental map, then distrbuting "images" along it to be read off whenever one again looks for the contents of that "place on the street."

---

* In the monograph (Duncker, 1945, p. 31) this particular case was printed as 267,276, which is obviously a typographical error.

38

The accompanying figure is a fictitious map of Gorky Street.

The method is to make a vivid "image" of successive things to memorize at successive locations. Then, later (minutes later, hours later, days later, weeks later, months later—and, in the case of Luria's mnemonist, who used a memorized "mental map," years later), check the locations on the map (in our simplified case, the printed map of Gorky Street). The images may come to mind and the objects to have been memorized will then be remembered. The method is the Gorky Street Algorithm.

For example, suppose one has this shopping list: milk, eggs, cake,

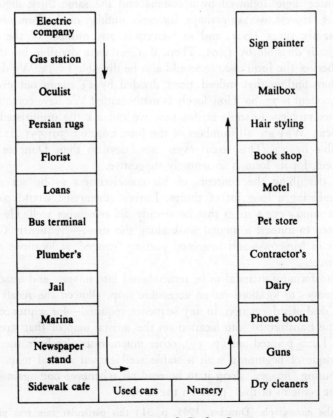

A fictitious map of Gorky Street.

chicken, bread, oranges, bananas, and caviar. One would "memorize" the list simply by making a vivid image of each item at successive locations, and "remember" the list simply by looking at the map when at the market, seeing what was at each location. One subject wrote, at the start:

ELECTRIC COMPANY imagining a cow being *milk*ed not by hand but by electrically run milking-machine.

GAS STATION getting new springs for the car so *eggs* would not be cracked as car travels on rutted roads.

OCULIST reaching for eyeglasses to be able to see the birthday *cake* well enough to count the candles.

PERSIAN RUGS picturing corn strewn on a rug so a *chicken* can peck at it to eat.

FLORIST going to consult a florist on what it is that has begun to grow on the old loaf of *bread*, because it does not look like penicillin.

LOANS the three-balls sign at the pawn shop is made of large *oranges*.

BUS TERMINAL the bus is filling up with monkeys eating *bananas*.

PLUMBER'S picturing a plumber removing *caviar* from a fish by suction using a small "plumber's helper."

At remembering time, one hour later, the subject checked the map and wrote this:

ELECTRIC COMPANY something is hooked up to wires—oh, yes, it is a cow's udder—the cow is giving milk. So, *milk*.

GAS STATION fixing the car—springs—jostling would break the eggs. So, it is *eggs*.

OCULIST I need glasses for seeing something—oh, yes, I am getting old and need glasses to count the candles on my birthday cake. So, it is *cake*.

PERSIAN RUGS what is that flying carpet there for? Oh, yes, for feeding chickens, with corn on the carpet. So it is *chicken*.

FLORIST the bread has gone bad and something like a flower is growing on it. So, it is *bread*.

LOANS (smiling) the pawnbroker has gone broke, having to pawn his globes and use oranges instead. So, it is *oranges*.

BUS TERMINAL the bus is full of . . . monkeys! Each has a banana. So it is *bananas*.

PLUMBER'S a plumber who does not know how to get caviar from salmon tries to suction the fish eggs out. Unpleasant! But, it is *caviar*.

JAIL . . . the jail is empty . . .

MARINA . . . nobody in the boat, on the lake, in the shop . . . I guess caviar was the last item, back at the plumber's.

In this little exercise, to demonstrate how a walk on Gorky Street takes place, the memorization was followed by delaying the remembering to an hour later. The list was an easy one. But the map had to be consulted to retrieve the objects with a feeling of assurance, and it was essential for retrieving them in the order in which they had been originally listed.

The following list of forty words was given to twelve Duke undergraduates to remember, using a 20-location map of "Gorky Street" put on the blackboard of the classroom. Thus the route would have to be taken twice. The list of words was read to them, with about 8 seconds between successive words. This set of words was used for a different purpose by Woodworth (1938, p. 10).

1. crush	15. gift	28. cabbage
2. umbrella	16. path	29. escape
3. sailor	17. grocery	30. irksome
4. cedar	18. satisfy	31. true
5. mischief	19. occasion	32. steep
6. salute	20. perverse	33. riot
7. school	21. nuisance	34. raisin
8. bashful	22. master	35. promise
9. ride	23. sulphur	36. apricot
10. clean	24. preach	37. stone
11. dark	25. minnow	38. doll
12. prospect	26. invite	39. overcoat
13. allow	27. soldier	40. eagle
14. captain		

I read the forty words to them, telling them to put images in Gorky Street addresses. Then I had them write out the forty items, numbering them one to forty, giving each its place in the order (which I thought would easily be read off from the number of the location from the start along the street).

Among the 12 subjects, the average number of words written down in their correct places in the sequence was 34 out of a possible 40. All but two of the 12 subjects had scores over 35. The other two subjects encountered disaster. One of them, call him Harry, got all the second twenty but only three of the first twenty. What had he done on the first walk down Gorky Street? Harry said that he had not walked down, nor made "images" but instead had imagined himself standing in the middle of Gorky Street, throwing those successive given words into successive places on the map. That did not work for Harry, which seems no surprise. The other subject who met trouble was a girl we'll call Penelope. Poor Penelope got *less* than 20 words of the 40 correctly written down. She had not played the game at all. She had listened to the words, tried rehearsing them to herself, doing all the things we do when we do not use a mnemonic device. Penelope said she just tried to remember, trying so hard she did not have the time to *notice* Gorky Street.

Needless to say, all performance plummets when the map is no longer available when making images and retrieving them. I invite you now to use portable memory maps that wisdom might lead some to carry about.

According to Yates (1966), the Greeks and Romans of classical times, as well as their intellectual descendants (at least till the time of Leibnitz), knew about an art of "artificial memory" which involved first committing to natural memory a large set of locations, and then making bizarre images of words or things to be remembered, putting them at those locations in the mind's eye. Some recent research work is interesting in the context of the Gorky Street Algorithm and the classical art of artificial memory. For instance, Jensen and Rohwer (1963) studied paired-associate learning in mentally retarded adults, supplying them with verbal mediators. Given "cat" as the stimulus and "toaster" as the response to be remembered to it—all in the context of "The *cat* popped out of the *toaster*"—give them cat and out comes toaster. Detailed analysis of related matters is found in Paivio (1965) and an interesting book by Norman (1969).

The ease with which amounts of material can be remembered on a walk on Gorky Street acutely raises the question of the structure of memory. The method presented here requires a map to be available for the processing into and out of images the objects at memorization and at recall time. Is natural memory of this type? The easy answer would say that all memory is of the same essence, that what you do explicitly on a walk down Gorky Street you do implicitly in natural memory. Thus the great advantage of the "coding" in the Gorky Street method is the availability of addresses where images are "stored" and from which they may be "retrieved."

The harder answer is that it remains entirely unknown what the relation between natural memory and "Gorky Street memory" is, just as details of the results in using the Gorky Street method will still have to be found out. The questions that remain are numerous: e.g., the number of items that can be "kept" at a single location on Gorky Street, the length of time in which items may be "stored" until retrieval, and the number of items that may be memorized per unit time.

The time it takes to form and retrieve an image may be rather important. Lockhead (1961) speeded up the time allowed for memorization in a different "one-trial-learning" task, that of Rock (1957). Performance dwindled when time was short. In Gorky Street it seems to take time to "form and locate the image," and in other analyses on these matters it may indeed be fruitful to suppose that cutting down time has its effect in the blocking of "rehearsal."

When Einstein lamented the force-feeding of knowledge to children, he supposed that knowledge was all right, but that too much kills curiosity. Yet, given curiosity still rampant, can there be too much knowledge available? No. But there can be too much knowledge intruding out of place. There is an old child's card game called "concentration" in which a deck of playing cards is spread out face down in some haphazard arrangement. Each player, in turn, chooses two cards —if they match (say, both are Queens) that player keeps those cards and goes again. If they do not match, the two cards are replaced from where they were turned over. Obviously, the trick for winning this game is to have a good memory. Children of about three years old win from adults at this, seldom missing matching a new card with one of the same kind that had once been overturned but replaced. But, when they are older, say five years old, they are no better at the game than we are—seldom remembering old cards. When they are younger, children do not verbally code the cards; later they do. Can we conclude that words intrude upon a better way that once was natural?

In spontaneous memorizing, the items to be remembered may have to somehow find their way to associates to tie them down on the dismal, unswept, dark foggy street on some backwater of your mind, some place on the wrong side of the tracks. It is a wonder that any memorizing ever gets done. Farfetched modern ideas that memory is like a hologram, or that it is coded in nucleic acid, or that it may be transferred by eating out another's brain may in the end be proved. In the meantime, we may play at the study of streets, learning to put recurrence of thoughts, *qua* memory, under some control.

A friend who wants to be anonymous did this experiment while he was coming down with Hong Kong flu, using a sentimental map of the street he had grown up on, as this protocol shows.

Unhappy at having agreed to do this "experiment," and coming down with the Hong Kong flu, I took a phone book and, checking consecutive sixth digits of seven-digit phone numbers, I made a little list of 20 one-digit numbers and set out to memorize them using this map, which is shown in the accompanying figure as a febrile rendering of the street I grew up on, West Avenue in Pawtucket, Rhode Island.

The twenty digits, in sequence, were:

1, 1, 6, 9, 5, 2, 2, 3, 5, 4, 1, 1, 4, 5, 8, 4, 9, 9, 7, 3.

Rattey's ice cream		Narragansett Park Race Track
Major's barber shop		
Fire station		⟶ To Boston
Home		Fish and chips
Bumpy's house		The monastery
The market		El. Gas Co. ballpark
The druggist		Dentist
⟵ To New York		The bully's house
South Woodlawn Elementary School		Piano lessons
Book store	Haunted house	Bicycle shop

A sentimental map of West Avenue.

The protocol of the retrieval of digits from that map was typed out.
Here it begins.

1. I am a rather fat little boy so I only can have *one* ice cream cone.
1. There is *one* person ahead of me, so I will not have to wait too long
   for my haircut.
6. They tell me there is a *six*-alarm fire. It must be very unusually
   exciting, for I had never heard of as many as six alarms for a fire
   before.
9. I now have permission to visit Bumpy's house whenever I like now
   that I am *nine* years old (or is it eight, or even seven?) No, I think
   it is nine, for I am so much older than Bumpy who is only . . .
5. Bumpy, who in reality is my own age, has become only *five* years old!
2. I have been sent to the market to get *two* bags of potatoes.
2. I then go to the druggist for *two* aspirins, for I expect a headache after
   this walk down West Avenue! Twenty digits, ha!
3. I am a man now, and Freud said, I seem to remember, that *three*
   represents the testes and penis, three good things to have now that
   one is a man and goes alone off to New York!
5. Here I am not too sure. Maybe it is four. No, it must be *five*, for I
   am in the fifth grade now, and that is Miss Broome's class, I believe.
4. I buy two books. . . . no! I buy four books, so the number is four!
   four! Not two, for I remember trying to think of a four-volume
   set of books, but can only think of sets of three volumes—but now
   I remember *The Alexandria Quartet* as what I should have
   thought to buy.
1. There is only *one* ghost in the haunted house; he is snappish because
   he is lonely.
1. At the bicycle shop the only cycle in view is broken so it might still
   be used as a unicycle; *one* wheel still turns.
?. Oh, the piano lesson is empty. I cannot remember anything, quite
   like it was indeed when I was a stupid child at boring piano lessons.
5. I do not want to think too much of Billy Hart, who was the
   school bully and used to terrorize me, so I just yell "Bully!" and
   notice it has *five* letters.
8. I am still unhappy from going to piano lessons where I forget
   everything and passing the bully's house, so in going to the dentist's,
   another unhappy affair, I fall into compulsive counting obsessions
   with appropriate symbolism; the number was *eight*, and I had noticed
   it was the number of letters in the word *dentist*, plus the gap like
   an extracted tooth where the door is drawn on the map.
4. The sun shines again, and I am freed. The bases are loaded, and I

am at bat, so there are *four* of us about to score, if the home run can only be made!

9. This is rather remarkable. What was the association? Three times three? A square of monks? I don't know, but the number *nine* seems to belong at the monastery; I seem to have put it there.

3. Another disaster! Fish and chips, all right, but what happened in that shop? I must not have made a good image. In fact, I seem to recall wondering how to make a sandwich of fish and chips, so I will hazard a guess that the number was *three*.

7. I think that I am going to get away from Pawtucket, and realize that would be heaven, which rhymes with *seven*, which is a lucky escape!

3. There are *three* bets at the races, win, place, and show.

		1	*2*
1	1	1	1
2	1	1	1
3	6	6	6
4	9	9	8
5	5	5	5
6	2	2	2
7	2	2	2
8	3	3	3
9	5	5	5
10	4	4	4
11	1	1	1
12	1	1	1
13	4	?	4
14	5	5	5
15	8	8	8
16	4	8	8
17	9	9	9
18	9	3	3
19	7	7	7
20	3	3	3

After the dotted line is my recall. I get the 13th and the 16th wrong! The 13th is the piano lesson where I cannot remember anything, but now, looking at the stimulus list, I remember the image I had formed was playing a four-hand piece, a duet with my ugly, dull piano teacher. I doff my cap to Freud again. The 16th was El. Gas Co. Ballpark, which we used to call El Gasco, assuming it to be Spanish and mysterioso. One of the marvelous Fourth of July bonfires that we gangs of kids made included roaming down to El Gasco and ripping out the rotten wooden bleachers, and bringing them to Slater Street Grammar School for the mammoth bonfire. I truly remember that the number to be remembered there was four, not eight, and once more I congratulate Freud!

But, all in all, 18 out of 20 is not so bad. I began by selecting the list at 10:15 this morning, and going for a short *real* walk, not thinking about that at all. Then at 10:30 I was back at my desk, going for the walk down West Avenue. By 11:30, everything up to the congratulation to Freud was typed, so now it is noon, after another walk, some phone calls about business matters, a cup of coffee. Time to go down West Avenue again, to see what I have lost of those damn digits.

Rattey: *one* cone. Major: *one* patron. Fire: *six* alarms. Home: *eight* (or is it nine?) years old. Bumpy: he's only *five*. Market: *two* potatoes. Druggist: *two* aspirin. New York: *three*, the symbol of masculinity. School: Grade *five*. Books: *four* volumes of Lawrence Durrell. Haunted house: *one* lonely ghost. Bicycle shop: *one* working wheel. Piano: *four*-hand duets with the hag. Bully: Billy has *five* letters. Dentist: *eight* teeth, one pulled out. El Gasco: *eight* players not four: we are not at bat, but I am pitching with the rest of the team, eight of them, in the field. Monastery: *nine* months, three times three, convoluted masculinity. Fish and chips: *three* layers in a sandwich. To Boston: lucky *seven*. Gansett: *three* possible bets.

Now I check these numbers: 1, 1, 6, 8, 5, 2, 2, 3, 5, 4, 1, 1, 4, 5, 8, 8, 9, 3, 7, 3. Again two mistakes! How can this be? Oh, horror! The numbers should be

1 1 6 9 5 2 2 3 5 4 1 1 4 5 8 4 9 9 7 3

but instead I have given

1 1 6 8 5 2 2 3 5 4 1 1 4 5 8 8 9 3 7 3

Ah, what confusion! Indeed, from the start I was nine years old, not eight years old, so home equals *nine*. All right, I have that now, I hope. But it needs to be fortified. I will be, henceforth, nine years old, with a baseball costume on, to remind me that there are nine on a team (but will this ruin El Gasco's eight *other* players?). El Gasco, I now find, should be four, not eight. In the original list taken from the telephone book, the number in that place in the sequence was four, but I falsely remember that I had made a mistake in thinking it was four, but instead it should be *eight*. I check back and forth, a victim of the psychopathology of everyday life! All along it should be *four*, and I still fail to understand why I thought at any time it was supposed to be eight! Muddled over that, I continue. For fish and chips I put down three for the layers of a sandwich, but see it should be *nine*. How come? So I was wrong the first time through at the 18th digit, saying it was three, but mistakenly typing nine when indeed the original number was nine. Henceforth, there will be as many sandwiches ordered in the fish and chips shop as there are layers in one sandwich, three times three equals *nine*! So, we must amend the score. The first time through I missed three, getting only 17 of the 20 digits correct. The second time through, again 17 correct, three errors.

I choose to stop this now, for indeed the headache comes, and I would that I had those two aspirins from that West Avenue druggist!

12:30 P.M., 12/16/68

I go for a brisk walk on the quadrangle, brisk because it is very cold—maybe the middle 20s, and I return here to this typewriter intent on typing out what I remember, *without consulting the map*. I began the walk at Rattey's, *one* (cone). There is the fire station which is *six* (alarms). At my house I am *nine* (years old), but next door poor Bumpy is somehow only *five* (years) old—perhaps the age he got his nickname by having a bicycle as a present delivered to his upstairs bedroom, and his testing it out by riding it downstairs—or so went the story as I remember it. At the market, *two* (potatoes), at the druggist's *two* (aspirin). At school I am in the *fifth* grade—as indeed I could hardly truly be at age 9. Oh, well, another tug at the edge of my mind that Freud lurks just around the corner perhaps. At the bookstore, *four* (books). At the haunted house, *one* (ghost). At the piano teacher's house, *four* (hands). At the monastery, *nine* (monks). At the bully's house, which I think I must have run past for I think it is before the monastery on this fictitious West Avenue, *five* (letters in this name). At the fish and chips place, was it three or was it nine—oh, yes, it was *three*—three-layer sandwiches, so *nine* (in all). At El Gasco, I am at bat, not pitching, so the number is *four* (on base). Going to Boston is *seven* (lucky!), and at the other end of U. S. Route 1 is New York; that is *three*. At Gansett racetrack, *three* (bets).

Seventeen locations with numbers recalled! Which are the three lost? Let me look at the list of locations, see what's missing. Ah, the barber shop, with one (patron) . . . the bicycle shop with one (wheel) . . . So, 19 and they all seem right. Where is that last, that missing 20th? Hilarious, Sigmund, are you listening? The frightful dentist! Where there are eight letters and a door like a missing tooth.

1:05 P.M., 12/16/68

Indeed, it seems that all the numbers are now correct in relation to their locations on West Avenue. But the locations are not remembered! The sequence is lost. Not like Luria's mnemonist's Gorky Street. But, indeed, I think I shall be perfect naming digits as I go along West Avenue now. Let's see!

1 1 6 9 5 2 2 3 5 4 1 1 4 5 8 4 9 9 7 3. Copying the correct list once more: 1 1 6 9 5 2 2 3 5 4 1 1 4 5 8 4 9 9 7 3. Grüss Gott!

1:12 P.M., 12/16/68

For a rather unsurprising reason, namely that I never remembered *anything* perfectly before, and 20 digits is thought to be *hard*, I now intend to go to the phone book again, select 20 new digits, say from the next-to-the-last digit of consecutive phone numbers randomly selected: 2 7 7 2 0 7 8 6 3 4 7 3 4 2 5 2 1 7 4 7.

Then, I retrieve the list:

At Rattey's I sit in a booth with a girl, ordering *two* sodas. At Major's I win the punchboard game, which is very lucky (equals *seven*). At the fire station I play checkers all day and never lose—again, lucky *seven*. At home we live in a three-decker tenement on floor number *two*. Bumpy has gone to be a psychologist at Harvard. How many boys are home —*zero*. It is really a lucky day; I order a half-dozen eggs but get *seven*. I, all of a sudden, come to *hate* the druggist, which rhymes with *eight*. To New York again, twice as potent—two times three equals *six*. At school I am now back to the third grade, a rather happy grade, *three*. At the bookstore I do buy *The Alexandria Quartet* (*four* books). At the haunted house there are good ghosts with whom I share *seven* eggs. The bicycle shop has a bicycle in addition to unicycle: two plus one equals *three*. At piano lessons I remember nothing again, but I assume it is old "*four*." The bully and I square off and fight it out at his house; he plus I equals *two*. The dentist, out back with a stinging beehive rhymes with *five*. At El Gasco, I am pitching and the call is no balls, *two* strikes. At the monastery, monotheism triumphs, yea verily God is *One*. There are some sickly french fries on the plate—*eight* of them. To Boston, but why? I think there are *two* of us in the car. At the races I win every race, very lucky even unto race number *seven*.

Dammit! I now see there were seven french fries, and four on the way to Boston. Eighteen out of twenty. Not too bad.

1:48 P.M., 12/16/68

It is now 2:00 P.M., 12/16/68, and I intend to stop this numbered walk on the street of my childhood. To bid it farewell, I now go down its

20 consecutive locations, putting down at each location, the two digits therein.

Location number	First run	Second run
1 Rattey's	1 cone for the fatty	2 sodas for me and her
2 Major's	1 patron being shaved	7 is the punchboard number
3 Firehouse	6 alarm fire	7 lucky checker games
4 Home	9 years old am I	2 is the floor for me
5 Bumpy's	5 is how old he is	0 are the boys at home
6 Market	2 potatoes please	7 eggs instead of 6!
7 Druggist	2 aspirin for maugre me head	8 rhymes with dislike
8 New York	3, let's go!	6, twice as good!
9 School	5th Grade, perhaps	3rd Grade, for sure
10 Book Store	4 for Lawrence	4 for Durrell
11 Haunted House	1 ghost lonely	7 have a scrambled feast
12 Bicycle Shop	1 unicycle	3 wheels on Uni + bi
13 Piano	4 hands duet	4 hands again
14 Bully	5 letters in name	2 fists, let's fight!
15 Dentist	8 letters + door	5 bees astinging
16 El. Gas Co.	4 men on base	2 strikes; bear down!
17 Monastery	9 monks	1 deity
18 Fish & Chips	9 layers of sandwich	8 droopy french fries
19 To Boston	7 is a lucky escape	4 on double date
20 Racetrack	3 bets at the window	7 winning races

Goodness! Forty-nine out of fifty! One extra bad french fry, for there are only seven at Fish & Chips. Oh, well. Enough.

2:18 P.M., 12/16/68

It is now 2:50 P.M., 12/16/68, and I just wondered whether the place that Freud is in all this is that he sketched out the rules of the game for making those images when you are not aware that you are making images! What I mean is this: When I chose an image, like I pick the digit 1 and "attach" it to Rattey's ice cream parlor on my map of West Avenue, everything is explicit and aboveboard—I think of *one* and of ice cream and of being a fat kid then, and think such a fat kid should surely have no more than one ice cream cone. But now take the case of remembering something —say that I was a fat kid, or that the local ice cream parlor was called Rattey's, or any old thing that pops into awareness without specific explicit rules for it to appear. Why does it appear? Freud supposed that, indeed, there were implicit rules, and he spelled them out. When we remember things without the use of an explicit West Avenue, our memory tends to be very faulty indeed. It seems to conform to illogical rules *a la* Freud, *plus* there are awful gaps in it. According to Freud and all others in that tradition, it is a map of affects that controls errors and mistakes, and even in this little protocol we can see the appeal of such an idea. Of course, with explicit maps and care in forming happy rather than dreadful images, these maps seem to show the way to the perfectibility of memory.

3:02 P.M., 12/16/68

It is 4:55 P.M., 12/17/68, and I sit on the edge of my bed after a day wracked c̄ ? Hong Kong flu? with very frequent stopping of the wheels of life.

Let me stumble on West Avenue, and see what I still remember.

	First	Second
1	1	2
2	1	7
3	6	7
4	9	2
5	5	0
6	2	7
7	2	5
8	3	6
9	5	3
10	4	4
11	1	7
12	1	3
13	4	4
14	5	2
15	8	5
16	4	2
17	9	1
18	9	6
19	7	4
20	3	7

Too tired to bother to see how it scored!!

5:00 P.M., 12/17/68

Let me test my Hong Kong flu list of 40 digits, see how I can retrieve it from West Avenue.

1. one (cone for fatso)
2. one (old shaver)
3. six (alarm fire)
4. nine (I am)
5. five (he is)
6. two (potatoes)
7. two (aspirin)
8. three (to get ready)
9. five (Mrs. Broom's grade)
10. four (Durrell volumes)
11. one (lonely spook)
12. one (unicycle)
13. four (-hand boredom)
14. five (letters in Billy)
15. eight (d-e-n-t-i-s-t + door)
16. four (on base)
17. nine (monks)
18. nine (layers in three BLTs)
19. seven (ah, heaven!)
20. three (possible bets)
21. two (romantic sodas)
22. seven (lucky punchboard)
23. seven (checker wins)
24. two (the second floor)
25. zero (Bumpy & bros. gone)
26. seven (eggs)
27. eight (hate, hmm!)
28. six (on the way)
29. three (whose grade?)
30. four (more "Alexandrians")
31. seven (eating the eggs)
32. three (bi- + uni-cycle)
33. four (-hands still)
34. two (fighting it out)
35. five (rhyme—beehive)
36. two (strikes called)
37. one (monotheistic)
38. seven (f.f.pot.)
39. four (double dating)
40. seven (all horses win)

I hope that I can find a way to stop going through this damned list. Forty digits! Okay, so I am pleased as punch.

8:15 P.M., 12/26/68

Let's see how it is a month later.

1. one
2. one
3. six
4. nine
5. five
6. two
7. two
8. three
9. five
10. four
11. one
12. one
13. four
14. five
15. eight
16. four
17. nine
18. nine
19. seven
20. three
21. three
22. seven
23. seven
24. two

25.	zero	33.	four
26.	seven	34.	two
27.	eight	35.	five
28.	six	36.	two
29.	three	37.	one
30.	four	38.	seven
31.	seven	39.	four
32.	three	40.	seven

4:45 P.M., 1/28/69

4
Recurrence and intelligence

Here is the first distemper of learning, when men study
words not matter.
FRANCIS BACON

William James took the discussion of genius out of the shadows
and into the laughter of sunshine. In part, he wrote, it is richness of
association and in part it is ignoring "old hat." James, in one of *his*
strokes of genius, brings confusion to the front. After all, he notes,
confusion is mistaking the wrong part of something for the thing,
while reasoning is taking the right part of something for the thing.
Therefore, both confusion and reasoning partake of the same essence.

I believe that the only difference between a muddle-head and a genius is
that between extracting wrong characters and right ones. In other words,
a muddle-headed person is a genius spoiled in the making. I think it will
be admitted that all *eminently* muddle-headed persons have the temperament of genius. They are constantly breaking away from the usual consecutions of concretes. A common associator by contiguity is too closely tied to
routine to get muddle-headed (James, 1890, p. 352).

As it is for muddle-heads and geniuses, so it is for madmen who
surpass a healthy man of unusual ideas. The schizophrenic in the raw
shows none of the restraint that normality has us draw a line around.
Arieti (1955, p. 183) writes of a schizophrenic that when he cannot
change himself any longer even in a neurotic way, he must change
reality. But since reality cannot really change, he must somehow see
"reality" in a changed way. So also does the scientist have to see reality
in a different way, to put knowledge in novel combinations to solve
formerly unsolved problems. He, too, has mechanisms at his passive
disposal that are inherent in his human nature—that the poetry and
the theories of a spontaneous sapient honey bee are not at all likely
to be like the poetry and the theories of a spontaneous sapient man.
Arieti wrote that the schizophrenic does not use ordinary (Aristotelian)
logic. "*Whereas the normal person accepts identity only on the basis of
identical subjects, the [schizophrenic] accepts identity based upon
identical predicates.*" Arieti specifically notes the use of identity based

53

on (1) predicates of quality, (2) predicates of spatial contiguity, and (3) predicates of temporal contiguity. The first concerns taking one thing for another when they share some concrete or abstract quality; the second concerns taking one thing for another when they lie in a similar place; and the third concerns taking one thing for another when they occur at a similar time. Concerning (1), one may form the hypothesis that the way to fix a broken automobile headlight is to apply knowledge gained from fixing a broken lamp (since they both have the quality of having illuminated but are now failing to do so). Concerning (2), one may form the hypothesis that what is true for a part of a thing is true of all the parts of a thing (the *pars pro toto* of traditional logic analysis). Concerning (3), one may form the hypothesis that the first of two events which occur in temporal pairs is the cause of the second event (the *post hoc ergo propter hoc* of traditional logical analysis).

Further, Arieti argues that "normal thought" is concerned with both the connotation and the denotation of a symbol; the schizophrenic is mainly concerned with the denotation and the verbalization and partially abandons connotation. This is not only characteristic of schizophrenic thought, but is said to be true of the organization of dreams—perhaps of daydreams and reveries, and surely of the mental play of man on the scent of creative insight.

It may not be eternally fruitless to inquire whether (1) is characteristic of man because he learns to imitate himself and others; (2) is characteristic of man once he learns about objects by taking them apart and putting them together; and (3) is characteristic of man as he notices the effect of what he does at one time on what occurs at a later time. Nor is it hard to believe that the power of the six words "Nymphs and shepherds dance no more" in startlingly and poignantly affecting man can be analyzed in terms of those words being resonated to by a deep part of man who has lost the hope and innocence and freedom of human childhood. But this consideration will take us too far afield at this point if carried further now.

There is a gamelike character of creative scientific work and it is amusing to describe the players. Creative scientists are studied by psychologists in Anne Roe's germinal *The Making of a Scientist* (1953) and Bernice T. Eiduson's *Scientists: Their Psychological World* (1962).

From these books one finds that creative scientists are intelligent, absorbed in their work, and oriented toward rejecting "old hat." From the work of Silvan Tomkins also comes the idea that there may be a rather consistent early childhood experience of creative scientists, in that they tend to have been made much of by their mothers and neglected by their fathers. And, coming from informal observations is another life-history event that often has occurred; when the person who is to become a creative scientist is an undergraduate, he is given an opportunity to work on an independent research problem. The fun of such independent work can "infect" a student with a love of independent finding-things-out that lasts. And lastly, quite often the very good scientist has been the student of a very good scientist in graduate school.

This last point is curious. What has a creative scientist learned?

Traditional education consists of the force-feeding of knowledge. One is taught how to speak and write, and later the formal discipline of language; how to do arithmetic manipulations, and later the formal discipline of mathematics; one may be taught substantive areas of knowledge—the facts of geography, of history, of economics, of the several sciences, and one is taught some of the local history and methods of inquiry in the several substantive areas. Along the way to an advanced degree in science, one is taught the formal system of logic and rules of procedure in the evaluation of information. And finally, one is taught a specific area of knowledge to be furthered by one's own Ph.D. dissertation. Under the best of regimens, one learns how to teach himself what one wants to know, and gains experience in the independence of mind required for pushing on when one does not know what is best to do next. Independence of mind and high motivation to push onward may be necessary, but they may not be sufficient. For illumination to occur, preparation must have occurred. Beveridge suggests wide reading in science, and while this may seem an inefficient way to prepare for working on a scientific problem, perhaps something necessary is learned in such reading. Is it necessary to learn strategies and general procedures that can be imported into a wide set of problems? Call these strategies "cognitive moves." It seems possible that the very good research scientist has picked up a set of "cognitive moves," and a motivated and intelligent student can learn them from such a teacher, even if neither of them has ever specifically formally stated them—

like every human child learns to imitate postures and attitudes of his parents without their being explicitly stated by any of the parties involved.

Wild talents, like Luria's mnemonist's talent for remembering, are not all that rare. Take mental calculators. Their skill is phased out by the onrush of industrialization. "Mental calculators may, like the Tasmanian or the Moriori, be doomed to extinction," wrote poor Aitken (1954). He had been one of those mental-calculation wizards, but came a day when he got one of those new-fangled electric desk calculators, and sad to say, he saw there was no need for his talent—the machines could do automatically what he did humanly. Wild talents will *always* be in danger of being understood; the algorithms underlying them will sooner or later be found. Machines, after all, are just realizations of algorithms for some action, be it simple or complex, easy or hard, amusing or dreadful.

Of course, once one realizes that rules can be found that let a machine do a human thing, one can hardly avoid the joyous realization that there *are* rules, and that we can work at making them clearer. We will be wise to remember that just because a mountain is there presents no necessity to climb it at once. Once Cyrus Eaton asked Thomas Edison, who also was hard of hearing, to perfect the hearing aid. Edison refused, saying, "I don't want to hear that much."

In our Gorky Street, we had built a form to put content, a little plenum of our own—the street is full of locations that are arranged in a sequence. Should someone come along and rearrange the contents of the street, the *sequence* of "memories" would be *ruined*. But a walk down Gorky Street, or any other attack at memorization is slow as molasses. To destroy memory by putting things out of order or sequence may turn out to be nature's way. In the simpler case of compressed time, the analysis of blocking thought and stopping speech is infinitely more accessible.

On television there used to be, and still may be, something called "The Buster Brown Show." It was a show for children that featured a puppet named Froggy, who would destroy speech. Typically, there would be some supposed expert giving a lecture. As the expert paused in the midst of speaking, Froggy would jump into the pause and say some words. The expert would resume speaking, but would incorporate Froggy's intrusion. Here is an example of this sort of thing.

EXPERT In order to make your garden grow in a spell of very dry weather . . . (pause) . . .

FROGGY Whether or not

EXPERT . . . whether or not, you want . . . what I am saying, of course, you want your garden to grow.

Speech is rather an elegant topic for studies of the blocking of behavior, for it is so surprisingly fragile. The delay of hearing one's voice as one talks, by about 300 milliseconds, devastates speech. The usual apparatus for this is a tape recorder with earphones that monitor the playback heads, with a device for lengthening and thus slowing down the path the tape takes from the recording head to the playback head. Try to say banana, one says banananana—that sort of thing, something like stuttering.

Something like stammering can be avoided sometimes by cutting out all auditory feedback from one's talking, say, by putting white noise into earphones to mask the hearing of one's speech. So, there is some change for good or ill in speech when one cuts out, or delays feedback to the ears. How about advancing it, toying with advanced auditory feedfront, rather than delayed auditory feedback? There are at least two ways for hearing what you say before you have yet said it. In Case I, you can record some passage into a tape recorder and then play back that recording slightly in advance of the next reading of that passage. In Case II, you can study the speech of a shadower—someone who repeats each sound emitted by the target-person as soon as he hears it. With practice, one can become proficient at this sort of shadowing, a trick taught at one's *peril* to one's children. The prime difficulty in the Case II experiment, when both the shadower and the target read aloud from some passage, is that while not much happens to the speech of the target, the shadower cannot follow his wish to stay a constant distance behind—he tends quickly to catch up and get in phase. Everyone, as a child, has had the same experience in recycling into phase when trying to sing rounds.

In an interesting experiment by Norman (1969), English words were read into one ear of a subject while he went along repeating them in a shadowing fashion. But simultaneously, digits were read into the subject's other ear. When tested on his memory for the digits, subjects remembered them soon after they were read to them, but if 20 seconds elapsed no memory for the digits remained at all.

Thought is at least as fragile as speech. Staying close to the paradigm of experiments on delayed auditory feedback, there are two terrible things to do that quite easily destroy thought. One is called semantic satiation and the other is "the stupid-reader effect." The first has long been known, and can be experienced by repeating over and over to yourself "Perth Amboy." Perth Amboy Perth Amboy Perth Amboy Perth Amboy Perth Amboy Perth Amboy Perth Amboy Perth Amboy, etc. Notice how the trappings of relevance and meaning fall from the name of that New Jersey town. Research on semantic satiation is reviewed and evaluated in a valuable article by Harriett Amster (1964). The second is a particularly distressing form of distraction (Crovitz, Schiffman, and Rees, 1967). You can have a person silently read along some easy material, but every little while you say aloud some word he has already read. Often all meaning will be gone from the reader, much like what we imagine happens to stupid people reading easy material and intelligent people reading difficult material. In semantic satiation, meaning is removed from words by the senseless repetition of them; in the stupid-reader effect, meaning is removed from a passage by, again, the senseless repetition of parts of it.

It is now time to describe an afternoon with the problem of enlisting volunteers for experiments upon them. In actual large-scale experiments done at American universities, the ordinary method for getting subjects into one's hands is to take advantage of the large course in introductory psychology, the students in which are made aware that they must be subjects in experiments as one of the requirements of the course. At the other extreme, for small-scale intensive experiments done in laboratories across the nation, the experimenter and his co-workers, all of whom may appear as authors of the eventual article, or anyway appear in a magnanimous footnote, are also the experiment's subjects. But "volunteers" who are made members of a press-gang may be inappropriate for some studies, and one's colleagues are too likely to guess the hypothesis. The best experiments are ones like the delayed auditory feedback experiments, where knowledge of what is going on is irrelevant. In such an experiment, subjects are temporarily reduced to ideal physiological preparations.

The association of repetition to speech and thought requires a special kind of experiment, but one that seems of some general value. The quintessence of repetition of each word that you speak is the experiment on delayed auditory feedback in which a variable tape-track recorder is used. But even that is far from perfect since one hears the feedback from what one has said, coming via the earphones, but also hears what one is saying at present, via bone conduction to the ears. In the stupid-reader effect, the experimenter does not repeat every word the subject has read, just some of them. Allied to the stupid-reader effect is the got-you effect, in which the intention to speak, the thought that runs the tongue, is destroyed.

In class one day, some undergraduates were told to tell a story, and observe the destruction of thought. One began, "There were three men on their way to Chatham . . . (pause) . . ." During the pause, the teacher said "Chatham," and the student boggled. He froze in amazed silence, having forgotten what he was going to say. Another student said, "I went downtown to the station and sat down at the lunch counter . . . (pause) . . ." During this pause, the teacher said, "I went," which also erased whatever was to follow—not just the speech, but the intention.

In the original studies of the boggling effect of tossing a word into a pause in speech, those who were boggled recovered from the feeling of shock to say, "You got me!"—whence came the name of this phenomenon.

The effect is rather hard to get to work, for the words tossed into the pause and the place in the time-course of the pause appear to make some difference. A large-scale experiment seemed to be in order, but since a subject would be spoiled—i.e., would be wary and busy marshalling defenses against distraction—after the first trial, the experiment would be very wasteful. One ought not to make a subject come to the lab for a 1-minute experiment. The problem is doing the experiment without having the hundred subjects come to the lab, or worse still, having the experimenter go to a hundred subjects.

An accessible means to solve that problem is the telephone. To get prepared for a real experiment, and to test the feasibility of the method, the experimenter called on the telephone to three people, one after the other—two secretaries and his wife. To each he said, "I am doing an experiment. What I want you to do is say one sentence about the First World War and then one sentence about the trees of North

Carolina." With stunning regularity, each "subject" paused between the war and the trees. The experimenter during the pause repeated the last two words that the subject had already said, and each subject went right back and repeated the first sentence and without pause rushed through the second sentence. What regularities might be waiting there?

How could one find out? The experimenter plans, some day, to put an advertisement in the newspaper that would go like this:

BE IN A PSYCHOLOGY EXPERIMENT IN YOUR SPARE TIME, IN THE COMFORT OF YOUR OWN HOME!
CALL 000-000-0000 NOW

One ghastly implication of this work is that it is rather easy to write paragraphs that cannot be understood. Just put words in the wrong order, the contents in the wrong form. This implication *ought to* catch you up short. It is obviously true that the sense of words is carried on the order of the words in English. It is similarly obvious that the sense of events is carried on the order of the events in Nature.

Events *cycling* on a plenum and language progressing in *serial order* are abstract ways of describing things that are hard to describe. Aristotle once defined form as *all of the boat but none of the wood*. There are formal eternal abstract events and then there are specific, ephemeral, concrete ones. In language, misspelled words are an accessible case of some interest, at the microscale of letters in a word (Lecours, 1966), for words demand a particular sequence to their letters.

Letters recur across words, and words recur across paragraphs. A lot of fun has been made of this *almost* obvious fact. For instance, Skinner (1957) insists that it is ridiculous to pay *any* attention to a formalist analysis of language, to say *nothing* of thought. He scoffs at Russell's observation that all we know of Shakespeare's mind is derived from recurring black shapes on white paper, and he does not look kindly at Molière's having noted that all that is beautiful in literature is to be found in the dictionary, as it is only the words that are transposed.

Skinner took one alternative to that flight through nonsense, supposing that the significance of words as they are generated is to be found in the relation between the verbal productions and their "controlling variables." Alas, this homily is not helpful, for the missing link between the presumptive "controlling variables" and literature is not yet the healthy child of an accomplished analysis, but remains the stillborn product of a pious wish.

Somewhat more accessible is "Project Poe," the search for an algorithm for writing scientific articles with dispatch, so that a machine could do it in a second or two, untouched by human thought after the algorithm is designed and the data are collected.

5

Project Poe

Sx hx, Jxhn! hxw nxw? Txld yxu sx, yxu knxw. Dxn't
crxw, anxther time, befxre yxu're xut xf the wxxds! Dxes
yxur mxther knxw yxu're xut? Xh, nx, nx—sx gx
hxme at xnce, nxw, Jxhn, tx yxur xdixus xld wxxds xf
Cxncxrd! Gx hxme tx yxur wxxds, xld xwl,—gx! Yxu
wxn't? Xh, pxh, pxh, Jxhn, dxn't dx sx! Yxu've gxt
tx gx, yxu knxw; sx gx at xnce, and dxn't gx slxw; fxr
nxbxdy xwns yxu here, yxu knxw. Xh, Jxhn, Jxhn, if yxu
dxn't gx yxu're nx hxmx—nx! Yxu're xnly a fxwl,
an xwl; a cxw, a sxw; a dxll, a pxll; a pxxr, xld gxxd-
fxr-nxthing-tx-nxbxdy, lxg, dxg, hxg, xr frxg, cxme
xut xf a Cxncxrd bxg. Cxxl, nxw—cxxl! Dx be
cxxl, yxu fxxl! Nxne xf yxur crxwing, xld cxck! Dxn't
frxwn sx—dxn't! Dxn't hxllx, nxr hxwl, nxr grxwl,
nxr bxw-wxw-wxw! Gxxd Lxrd, Jxhn, hxw yxu dx
lxxk! Txld yxu sx, yxu knxw—but stxp rxlling yxur xf
an xld pxll abxut sx, and gx and drxwn yxur
sxrrxws in a bxwl.

EDGAR ALLAN POE, "X-ING A PARAGRAB"

Turing asked a good question; namely, given two question-answerers,
one a person and the other a machine, how could the question-asker
tell which was which? Were a machine to be programmed in some
manner so that it could fool a question-asker, the Turing question takes
an interesting turn. Given two people as the question-answerers, how
could the question-asker tell which was which, or even whether there
was one answerer or two? In fact, how can one tell if it is one or *n*
people giving answers? The experiment can be done rather easily in
the files of a psychology service in a psychiatric hospital by taking
some clinical test, say the Thematic Apperception Test, or the Ror-
schach, and assembling protocols for this experiment. One might take
Question 1 from one patient's answers, Question 2 from another, Question 3 from another, and so on. Could you tell whether the answers
came from one or more than one patient?

I have the opinion of three clinical psychologists to whom I often
speak freely. Of course, I expected their curiosity would be aroused
to their immediately setting out to do the necessary experiment to

answer the question with data. However, they are too busy to do more than express opinions. One was quite sure that one could do very well at distinguishing between the average "honest" protocol and the average "rigged" protocol. Another was quite sure the discriminability between the two kinds of protocol would be extremely poor, and chance results would come from such a study. The third was fairly certain it would not be chance nor perfection, but somewhere halfway between. This variant of the Turing question has not been put to experimental test as yet; everyone has other things to do.

Computers now are programmed both to perform experiments and to analyze the data from the experiment according to articulated rules. This takes care of the Method and Results section of a normal scientific article, untouched by the experimenter's hands. For the machine to be the author of the article that will describe the experiment and its findings, there must still be composed an Introduction that states the hypothesis and a Discussion that explicates the significance of the findings in terms of other work in the particular domain of the present article.

We could set out to design a form of an article that would fit any piece of work. I suppose that some industrious technician might put a machine to work analyzing out the similarities and differences in all pieces of scientific or engineering work, then equipped with it, set out to let the computer grind out the articles. Better, it seems to me, would be to sketch the work that seems to me needed to bring an all-round discoverer-computer into the game, and then go into new domains that are open for people now—i.e., new problems that are both so interesting and so muddled that as yet there is no foreseeable route to their solution.

On the broad scale of articles, certain words recur. On the compressed scale of words, letters recur. Often.

Edgar Allan Poe wrote a story entitled "X-ing a Paragrab." It tells of a vituperative rivalry between the editors of two newspapers that culminated in Editor A composing a mocking paragraph just full to overflowing with the letter "o" but the rival removing his stock of "o's" from the "case." Said Editor A's foreman, "Just stick some other letter in for *o*, nobody's going to read the fellow's trash, anyhow." So when the copy called for an *o*, the printer's devil decided, "I *shell* have to *x* this ere paragrab," and so it came out with *x* for every *o*.

On November 24, 1967, a letter was published in *Science* by Reynolds (1967); it complained about the jargon in that generalist's journal. He reported that he began circling the words he did not know, then switched to circling the words he *did* know—arriving at just articles, prepositions, relative pronouns, auxiliary verbs, and modifiers. But, alas, the substantive nouns were jargon and thus opaque to the mind's eye.

We select a sample of scientific articles from *Science*. Articles therein span the whole range of disciplines recognized as "science," and they lie together as weekly strange bedfellows. We select as paragrabs to analyze, the introductory "abstracts" from 100 consecutively printed reports from a recent volume of *Science*.

There are two kinds of words in these abstracts: words that might appear in *any* abstract of a scientific article (call them y) and words that are specific to particular articles—having to do with content, not form (call them x). Consider this abstract made up out of whole cloth for this purpose:

Abstract. The discovery by Columbus of a new land beyond the western ocean is compared to other geographical innovations. The technique of ocean navigation was basic to several known voyages, and an improvement in navigation ability might follow from use of the compass and astrolabe. Measurements of the direction of the North Pole in relation to the morning star are described for seventeen mid-ocean sites.

The y-form words remain when the x words, the content ones, are x-ed from the paragrab. If we substitute for the x-ed words a number that represents the number of x words, the x-ed paragrab becomes this:

The discovery by (1) of a new (1) beyond the (2) is compared to other (2). The technique of (2) was (1) to several known (1) and an (1) in (2) might follow from use of the (1) and (1). Measurements of the (1) of the (2) in relation to the (2) are described for (3).

Summing, $x = 23$ and $y = 41$. Consider a nondimensional number that is

$$(1) \quad \text{Poe Number} = \frac{100x}{y}$$

so in this dummy paragrab, Poe Number $= 2,300/41 = 56$. Obviously, for a paragrab with as many x-ed out words as remaining words,

(2) Poe Number when $x = y = 100$,
and when the number of x-ed out words is very large in comparison to the number of "general" or "formal" words, the Poe Number would be increasingly large. In general, as the number of generally applicable words increases in relation to the number of words specific to a particular article, the Poe number goes from plus infinity to zero.

Consider filling in our same dummy paragrab with *different* content words. For example:

The discovery by *Euclid* of a new *geometry* beyond the *empirical method* is compared to other *deductive schemes*. The technique of *axiomatic statement* was *familiar* to several known *Egyptians*, and an *extension* in *geometric capability* might follow from use of the *geometry* and "*algebra*." Measurements of the *modeling* of the *Pythagorean theorem* in relation to the *geometric proof* are described for *analogous algebraic equations*.

This rather stilted paragrab would perhaps have been seen by Descartes as an amusing, but trivial, abstract for an announcement of the analytic geometry.

And so it goes. The reader is invited to amuse himself by making, and then filling in, the blanks in works that might appeal to him for some reason.

There is a *little* room for art in x-ing a paragrab now, for indeed there is never total agreement on the problem of distinguishing appearance from reality, or content from form. I particularly call your attention to the second word of the paragrab, "discovery." Is it a form word or a content word? I have treated it as a form word. If it is treated as a content word, and x-ed out, an added degree of freedom is gained, for good or ill.

A sample was taken of 100 consecutive report abstracts from a recent volume of *Science*. The figure on the next page indicates a plot of x by y. In this small sample of abstracts from small reports in *Science*, where a report is about 2000 words in length, Poe Numbers occurred from Poe Number 144 to Poe Number 42. The mean Poe Number was 80; the median was 77.

Through Poe Numbers all literary products become comparable, for you could x Einstein with the same x-er as you x *Love's Labour's Lost*. Surely, within science, it is immediately possible to embark on a

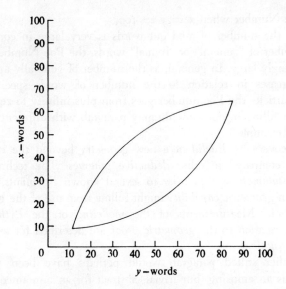

An envelope that contains the pairs of x-words and y-words
in 100 consecutive abstracts of reports from *Science*.

campaign of invidious comparisons between articles across disciplines,
across journals, or even, horror, across laboratories!

Consider some extreme paragrabs. Here are six with extreme Poe
Numbers:

1. Poe Number = 161

(1) between (5) and (7) the relative (1) of (1) in (2); between (4)
and (6) a (2) with (2) to have (1); after (5) again (2). The (1) ability
of the (2) shows that the (1) capacity for (1) operations exists (1) than
previously acknowledged.

2. Poe Number = 150

(1) of the (5) at least (3) were found in (4) in (3) of (2) in (3).
They readily (1) in the (1) and have since (1) into (3).

3. Poe Number = 124

(1) of the (4) and other (3) and (2) were found in (2) from (3) with a (2) of (4) or (3) on the (2) of (1). In addition, all (2) produced an increase in the percentages of (4) of (1) and of (2).

4. Poe Number = 53

A graphic and statistical comparison of major trends in (2) representative of (6) and (1) indicates a highly significant correlation for most (1) intervals between (1) and (2). This is suggestive of similarities in trends of (2) on the (2).

5. Poe Number = 33

The proposition that (2) of (2) may involve formation of (2) with specific (3) has recently been advanced. However, the primary data presented accord more quantitatively with the presumption of a (2) and furnish no evidence for the existence of the (3) which *are essential to the* proposed interpretation.

6. Poe Number = 37

(2) has provided the first direct (1) analysis of the (2). In addition, the amount of (2) was measured. More than (3) were taken, and a variety of scientific data were obtained.

A sample of 12 different reports from *Science*, the first dozen in a recent issue, was used for a study of the relationships among the Poe Numbers of "abstracts" and of the full article it preceded.

Table 4 shows the Poe Numbers for the 12 abstracts and the 12 full reports, exclusive of all tabular or illustrative material, the title and the notes and references—in other words, the report-writing itself.

In this sample, the median Poe Number for the abstracts is about 80; for the full reports, it is about 50. To put it in integer numbers, the median number of words in the body of the report was 1,200; 400 of them get crossed out; 800 of them remain as the form on which to hang the specific contents that distinguish one article from another.

As a final exercise in x-ing paragrabs, here are four reports* from

---

* The reports are Crovitz, H. F., Differential acuity of the two eyes and the problem of ocular dominances, *Science*, 1961, 134, 614; Crovitz, H. F., and

4

Poe numbers for twelve reports and their abstracts

Full report	Abstract
39	43
39	70
45	70
47	106
48	71
48	66
51	93
56	91
57	89
61	59
69	90
77	132

Science in which each *y*-word is unchanged and each *x*-word is now printed in italics. None of the illustrations, figures, tables, references or notes are included—such things, of course, are *x*, not *y*. Nor should these reports be considered typical—they are shorter than the average and all are from my work in vision.

1. *Differential Acuity* OF THE *Two Eyes* AND THE PROBLEM OF *Ocular Dominances*

Abstract. While it has long been thought that no relationship exists between the *eye* of *greater visual acuity* and the *eye favored* in *sighting*, the data collected suggest the need for a re-examination of this issue. *Sighting-dominance* and *acuity-dominance* were associated. In addition, most *individuals* tested showed *acuity-dominance* of the *left eye*.

In a systematic discussion of types of *ocular dominance*, *Walls* (1) differentiated between two which are commonly considered to be independent, namely, *sighting-dominance* (*one eye is consistently aligned* with

Lipscomb, D. B., Binasal hemianopia as an early stage in binocular color rivalry, *Science*, 1963, *139*, 596-597; Crovitz, H. F., Köllner effect and suppression of the view of an eye, *Science*, 1964, *146*, 1329-1330; Crovitz, H. F., and Schiffman, H., Visual perception and xerography, *Science*, 1968, *160*, 1251-1252. Copyright 1961, 1963, 1964, and 1968 by The American Association for The Advancement of Science. Reprinted here with permission of the publisher.

a *near point* when *sighting* or *pointing* at a *far point*) and *acuity-dominance* (*one eye* has greater *visual acuity* than the other). In this laboratory both kinds of *dominance* were measured in a large sample of *college students*. This paper reports the frequency of *left* versus *right acuity-dominance* and the association of *sighting-dominance* and *acuity dominance*.

Visual acuity was measured with a *Bausch & Lomb Ortho-Rater*, which measures *far acuity* and *near acuity* separately (2). For two *subject* groups one *eye* shows greater *acuity* than the other, that is, *acuity-dominance*. These groups consist of *subjects* in which (i) one *eye* shows greater *acuity* at both *far* and *near viewing distances*, and (ii) the *eyes* show equal *acuity* at one *distance*, but differential *acuity* at the other *distance*. Since testing of the *acuity* of the *left eye* follows testing of *both eyes together* and of the *right eye* (for both *near* and *far* conditions), the possibility of a *practice* effect favoring higher *left eye acuity* scores exists. To investigate this possibility, I tested 80 *college students*, with sequence changed so that the *right eye* tests were last in each *viewing* condition and, therefore, any *practice* effect would favor the *right eye*. In this sample, as in previously tested ones in which the usual order was used, mean *left acuity* was greater than mean *right acuity*, and there were more *left acuity-dominant* than *right acuity-dominant subjects*.

The question of an association between *sighting-dominance* and *acuity-dominance* was studied by *Gahagan*, who used a different measure of *visual acuity* (4). While he concluded that the two *dominances* are independent, a trend appeared in his data which could support the opposite conclusion. For those *subjects* showing *acuity-dominance*, of 63 *right sighting-dominant subjects* 54 *percent* were *right acuity-dominant*, and of 21 *left sighting-dominant subjects* 62 *percent* were *left acuity-dominant*. A re-examination of *Gahagan's* published data taken in conjunction with the data from my own studies suggests an association between the two *ocular dominances*. Table 1 shows the number of *subjects* showing each combination of *acuity-dominance* and *sighting-dominance*. A χ^2 *test* of *independence* was made ($\chi^2 = 9.59$; $p < .01$).

Inspection of Table 1 clarifies the finding of a prevalence of *left acuity-dominance*. Among *right sighting-dominant subjects*, *right* and *left acuity-dominance* are equally common. However, among *left sighting-dominant subjects*, *left acuity-dominance* is considerably more frequent than *right acuity-dominance*.

These data imply that to the extent that a sample consists of *left sighting-dominant subjects*, *left-acuity* would occur in more than half of the sample. Further, the data imply that in studies in which there is *monocular viewing* with the possibility of *acuity* being relevant, an index of the *different acuity* of the *two eyes* should be obtained, since it can no longer be assumed that *left* and *right acuity-dominance* will be equally distributed. In order confidently to generalize from these results it is suggested that (i) populations other than *college students* be sampled, and (ii) indices of *acuity* other than *Ortho-Rater scores* be obtained.

The clear demonstration of a bias favoring *left acuity-dominance* related to *sighting-dominance* may assist in the development of a valid conceptualization of the origin of *ocular dominances* and related *perceptual* events. The basic question of the origin of *ocular dominances* remains unanswered, and can be expected to remain so barring *developmental* studies.

2. *Binasal Hemianopia* AS AN EARLY STAGE IN *Binocular Color Rivalry*

Abstract. *Fifty* years ago Köllner reported that the *initial fleeting sensation* in *binocular color rivalry* is a *bipartite color field* such that the *color* presented to the *left eye appears* to the *left* of the *color presented* to the *right eye*. A method is described for *maintaining* such *quasi hemianopia* for *long periods* of *time*.

What will be *seen* when *discrepant stimulation* is applied to *corresponding* parts of the *two retinas*? *Woodworth* addresses this question and outlined the *responses* he felt the *brain* makes to such a *conflict* of *cues*: "It might *disregard one retina* and *respond* only to the *other*; or it might *respond* to the *combination* in several ways: by *fusion* of the *monocular fields*, by *seeing* one through the other, or where possible, by getting a *depth effect*" (1). Generally, the well-accepted notion of the *binocular* relation is that when the *monocular stimuli* cannot *merge* to form a *single, integrated percept*, and when the *stimuli* before one *eye* do not *dominate* completely, the *left-eye view alternates* over *time* with the *right-eye view*. This is generally granted even when the *neuroanatomy* of the *hemidecussating human visual system* is explicitly recognized and the assumption has to be made that in some unknown way each *eye* remains a *separate functional unit* as it *contributes* to the *binocular* result (2).

This concept of the *binocular relation* is not completely correct. The facts which it ignores were reported *half a century* ago, but so far as we know, they appear in no *modern treatment* of the problem. *H. Köllner*, at *Leipzig*, was interested in *nasal-temporal differences* in *vision*. He recognized that the *temporal fields* are larger than the *nasal fields* in *man*, and asked whether they might be *predominant* even in the *mutual visual field*. His paper reported observations of *binocular color rivalry* (3). It is well known that when *one eye* is *shown one color* while the *other eye* is *shown* a *spatially congruent* different *color*, the *two colors* will either *fuse* into *one*, or *one color* will alternate with the other over *time*. However, *Köllner* noted that the *initial sensation* was of a *bipartite field* of color, whereby the *color* before the *left eye appeared* to the *left* of the *color* before the *right eye*. That is, at *first*, sensation corresponds to *stimulation* from the *temporal visual field* only; this suggested to *Köllner predominance* of the *crossed fiber visual afferent* system.

Köllner's method is very simple. A *red glass* is *held* before the *left eye* and a *blue glass* is *held* before the *right eye*. When the *eyes* are *opened* one *fixates* the *center* of a *white surface*. *One sees red* to the *left* of *fixation* and *blue* to the *right* of *fixation*.

Since *rivalry* or *fusion quickly* takes the *place* of the *initial sensation* of the *bipartite color field*, some *practice* may be necessary in *observing* the *phenomenon*. We have found it easier to *observe* if the *eyes* are *open* only a *moment*. We came across *Köllner's* paper after completing a *tachistoscopic* study of *binocular color rivalry* in which we found that the most common *sensation* at a *duration* of *exposure* of 100 *msec* is a *bipartite color field* where the *stimuli* in the *nasal visual field* are not *seen*. This can be taken as a replication of *Köllner's* effect (4).

We have also found that when a *thin strip* of *black tape* is *placed* vertically down that *part* of each *glass corresponding* to the *fovea*, and *fixation* is *maintained* so the *strips* are *seen* as *one*, the *colors nasal* to the *strips* are not *seen* at all for *several minutes*. By this *simple method* an *apparent binasal hemianopia* is established in the *color fields*, similar to that *occurring initially*, but allowing study for *prolonged periods*. *Rotation* of the *strips* changes the *spatial* characteristics of the *color field*, which now *remains bipartite* in nature, generally without *fusion* of the *colors* over the *whole field* or *suppression* of *one eye*. When the *strips* are *placed horizontally*, then *rivalry* or *fusion* does occur.

The immediate purpose of this communication is to call attention to *Köllner's effect*. It must play a role in an adequate description of the *binocular relation*. The usual question has been what the *brain* can do when *discrepant stimuli* are *presented* to *corresponding areas* of the *two eyes*. The observations reported here represent an unexpected answer. The puzzling questions are these: what is the mechanism which controls *initial suppression* of the *nasal fields*, and why is the *sensation* of a *bipartite color field prolonged* when the *strips* are *presented?* The further puzzling question of the *means* by which one whole *eye* later comes to be *suppressed* also remains unanswered (5).

72

3. Köllner EFFECT AND *Suppression* OF THE *View* OF AN *Eye*

Abstract. *Köllner's* discovery of *binasal hemianopia* as an early stage in *binocular color rivalry* is extended to the study of the subsequent *suppression* of the *color seen* by *an eye*. The *Köllner* effect is one of the *five two-color configurations* that occur initially, and through which *total suppression* develops by the *visible expansion* of one of the *colors*. However, *suppression* sometimes occurs without a *two-color* phase.

When corresponding areas of the two *retinas* of a *subject* are exposed to different *colors* there may be *binocular color* mixture. When this does not occur, there is *binocular color rivalry*, characterized by the alternation of *suppression* of the *view* of the *left* and the *right eye*. The popular theory is that the *brain employs suppression* "as a *psychic* means of *escape* from *conflict*" (1). It is not known how "*the brain*" accomplishes *suppression*, nor how *suppression* of the *view* of the *eye* occurs during *binocular color rivalry*.

Köllner first reported that the *colors presented* to both *eyes* are both partly *visible* at first—that is, early *suppression* is incomplete. He found that before the *view* of one *eye* becomes *suppressed* something like *binasal hemianopia* happens: one *sees* a *split field* with the *left-eye color* appearing to the *left* of the *right-eye color*. This *sensation* is the *Köllner* effect (2). We now know that it depends in part on the size of the *retinal areas stimulated*. For areas subtending as little as 1° and 2° of *visual angle*, the reverse *Köllner* effect is more common: the *left-eye color* appears to the *right* of the *right-eye color* (3). To complicate matters, there are three other *two-color configurations* that are sometimes reported when *exposure duration* is short (a *tenth of a second*). They are *frames* (one *color* appears surrounding a *central area* of the other *color*), *stripes* (one *color* appears in a *vertical stripe* between *two stripes* of the other *color*), and *layers* (one *color* appears in a *horizontal band* above a *band* of the other *color*). A surprising fact is that only these *five two-color configurations* have appeared often in our studies.

The *two-color configurations* are related to the subsequent full *suppression* of the *color shown* to one *eye*. Some *subjects* in a pilot study *sketched* with *colored crayons* the "*stages*" that occurred when the *color square* was presented continuously for a few *seconds*. Their *sketches* indicated that often the *two-color configurations* remain *visible* until full *suppression* of one *color* occurs, and that the *color* that comes to occupy all the *perceptual* space often does so by *visibly expanding* from its location in the early *two-color configuration*. I have investigated the extent to which the first full *suppression* of one *color* develops through a *visible spatial incursion* of one *color* into the area *formerly occupied* by the other *color*, and the relative frequency at which such *expansion* occurs through each of the *five two-color configurations*.

Twelve college students viewed a *red square* with one *eye* and a *green square* with the corresponding area of the other *eye* in the apparatus used for previous studies (3,4). The duration of *exposure* was 3 *seconds*. There were *six* trials with each of the *four squares* differing in size: they *subtended* from 2° 12′ to 6° 08′ of *visual angle*, and the order of presentation was counterbalanced. After each observation period the *subject* reported the initial *appearance* of the *colored square*, and the changes in the *colored square* ending with *the appearance* of the full area in only one *color* (in cases in which the initial report was of only one *color*, which occurred for about *half* the trials, the first full *suppression* of interest was the *suppression* of that *color* as the other *color* became *dominant*). The experimenter coded the reports with respect to whether the change that occured was a *spatial incursion* of one *color* and, if so, whether the *incursion* was an *expansion* of a *color* from a *location* typical of one of the *two-color configurations* (5). For example, a *color* might *expand* through the Köllner effect (with the *left-eye color expanding* from *left* to *right*), the reverse Köllner effect (with the *left-eye color expanding* from *right* to *left*), *frames* (with one *color expanding* from all the *borders* into the *center*), *stripes* (with one *color expanding* from the *left* and *right border* into the *center*), or *layers* (with one *color expanding* from the *upper* or the *lower border*).

Table 1 shows the frequency of occurrence of each type of development of *suppression* of one *color*. There was no significant difference between *stimulus* sizes; data from all trials are pooled. For over 80 percent of the trials *suppression* occurred through an *apparent incursion* of one *color* so that it took over the "former *territory*" of the other *color*. Most types of development of *suppression* were reported by most *subjects*, indicating that the discovery of a *visual syndrome* in which only one type of *two-color configuration* occurs might prove of special interest. Apparently such a discovery has been made: *patients* with *strabismus* and *anomalous retinal correspondence* have been reported to *see* a *color rivalry target* as conforming to the Köllner effect for *patients* with *exotropia*, and conforming to the reverse Köllner effect for *patients* with *esotropia* (6).

For the *subjects* in the present study, on some trials one *color* was reported to *dissolve* uniformly, allowing the other *color* to be *seen*. But the *color* to be *dominant* usually *expanded* through one of the *five two-color configurations*. This appears to be the relevance of the Köllner effect, first reported 50 *years* ago, to the more general problem of *visual suppression*. The mechanisms

74

that underlie the *two-color configurations* and that determine the *flow of color* within them remain unknown.

4. *Visual Perception* AND *Xerography*

Abstract. An *electrostatic copying machine* was used to model the *perception* of *simultaneous brightness contrast.* Such a model may assist the study of *sensory inhibition* by permitting the study of *complex situations* as they are transformed by rules similar to those at work in *neural integration.*

A *century* ago *Mach* showed that in *human vision perceived brightness effects* are related to the *second derivative* of the *physical luminance distribution* of the *stimulus* and described what are now known as *Mach bands* (1). Even though the *stimulus distribution* contains no *discontinuities*, the *observer* may still *experience clearly demarcated stripes* or *bands. Ratliff* has pointed out that a similar phenomenon occurs in such *physical optical systems* as the *xerographic process* (2). We think that this coincidence is a fortunate one, for it allows one *system* to be used as a model of the other.

A hallmark of *xerographic copies* is the *"edge-only* effect*"* whereby only the *edge* of *wide areas* is *copied. Grundlach* has described methods for obviating this *Mach-bandlike* effect (3). *Broad areas* are *uniformly charged* on the *xerographic plate*, but they can be transformed into *an array of dots or lines* which are then *developed* by *edge-fields*, through *masking* the *original stimulus* during *projection*, through *selectively discharging* the *plate surface*, or through *initially charging* the *plate* in a *screen pattern.*

We may compare these techniques to ones that have been discovered in the history of *vision* research for affecting the *visibility* of *contrast* effects: the dependence of the *perceived brightness* in one *visual-field location* on the *brightness* in another *location*. With a *stimulus* such as that shown in Fig. 1 a classical demonstration of *simultaneous brightness contrast* in *human vision* is possible. The *stimulus* is a *ring* of *medium gray (Munsell N5)* on a *background half somewhat lighter (Munsell N6)* and *half somewhat darker (Munsell N4)*. The *photograph* gives a fairly good *picture* of the original *stimulus*, in which the *background* measured *9 cm high* and *12 cm wide* with a *ring 1 cm wide* and *6 cm* in *diameter* at its *outside edge* placed in the *middle* of the *background*. Few *observers see* any *lightening* of the *ring* on the *dark side* or any *darkening* of the *ring* on the *light side* of the original *stimulus*. Similarly, there is no substantial difference in *brightness* between the two *halves* of the *ring* in a *xerographic copy* of the original *stimulus* (Fig. 2). Figure 2 illustrates, however, the *edge-only effect* of *xerography.* The *electrostatic office dry copier* used was a *Xerox Model 2400*.

Woodworth described the methods that can be used to make *simultaneous brightness contrast* quite *obvious* in such a *stimulus* as that *photographed* in Fig. 1 (4). His account combines clear method with dubious theory. He notes that *ordinary viewing* is likely to give slight *contrast* effects. However, *covering* the *whole stimulus* with *white tissue paper* or *gauze* makes the *contrast* striking, and even *holding* the *stimulus close* to the *eye* so that *contours* and *texture* are out of *focus* will favor the effect because the *"field is deprived* of *object character."*

When a *woven fiberglass screen,* 20 *squares per inch,* is *placed* over the *original stimulus* there is a *vivid perceptual contrast* effect. The *half* the *ring* on the *dark side appears lighter* than the *half* the *ring* on the *light side.* Now we are prepared to consider a *xerographic copy* of the *original stimulus taken while it was covered* by the *fiberglass screen.* This *xerographic copy* is *photographed* in Fig. 3. Now indeed the *half* the *ring* on the *light side* is *copied darker* than the *half* the *ring* on the *dark side.* The difference in the *halves* of the *ring* is an *objective* difference.

We began with a *stimulus* which was carefully chosen to show no great difference in the *induced brightness* of the *halves* of the *ring* for the *eye* as compared to the *xerographic copier.* We *added* to that *stimulus* a *screen* that made the *halves* of the *ring* different in *brightness; in perception* the difference is a consequence of *subjective response* to the *workings* of *complex interactions* in *neural networks* behind the *retinal surface,* whereas in the *xerographic copy* it is a consequence of the *objective* effects of *electrostatic* fields in the *xerographic plate* which are mapped in the *xerographic copy.*

The fun of *x*-ing a paragrab is the fun of confronting the bare form of thought without having arbitrary details get in the way. Is that a way to learn the significance of those "arbitrary details" which, of course, are the wood of the boat, the necessary concepts of a science? But it is all in words, which is annoying.

Someone is likely to be able to transcend the verbal form used in this study of the plenum. One possibility might be to transform all problems into mathematics. Symbolism came rather late to mathematics itself. Bell (1945, p. 100) remarks that even the *Algebra* of al-Khowarizmi, which was one of the Hindu-Arabic books that reawakened the West from the dark ages, was all in the form of words. For example:

What must be the amount of a square, which, when twenty-one dirhems are added to it, becomes equal to the equivalent of ten roots of that square? Solution: Halve the number of the roots; the moiety is five. Multiply this by itself; the product is twenty-five. Subtract from this the twenty-one which are connected with the square. The remainder is four. Extract its root; it is two. Subtract this from the moiety of the roots, which is five. The remainder is three. This is the root of the square which you required and the square is nine. Or you may add the root to the moiety of the roots; the sum is seven; this is the root of the square which you sought for, and the square itself is forty-nine.

In modern dress this is the problem of finding x when $x^2 + 21 = 10x$. The solutions, of course, are 3 and 7. The problem was originally translated by E. Rosen in 1831, even at which date it was impossible to get along with bad symbolism.

Lavoisier rescued chemistry from the form of words and helped to put it into the form of symbols. This may have served to smooth the way of chemists who followed. However, a symbol replacing a word is not enough. Ramon Lull used notation, after all, back in the 13th century. To quote from Peers (1929, p. 64),

If in Thy three properties there were no difference . . . the demonstration would give the D to the H of the A with the F and the G as it does with the E, and yet the K would not give significance to the H of any defect in the F or the G . . . therefore the H has certain scientific knowledge of Thy holy and glorious Trinity.

A fresh key to the notation was given by Lull at the start of each chapter of *The Book of Contemplation*.

At any rate, if the problem is to generate appropriate *action* in literate human problem-solving, words may be convenient right now. When it comes to *getting rid* of words, beyond the paragrab is the palimpsest. In *x*-ing a paragrab one could cross out content words, saving form. In a palimpsest one does not save anything but the paper, scratching out the content, the form, and all of the ink. In days when paper or other writing material was in short supply, one got rid of what was on a writing surface and began again.

A variant of these methods consists of leaving the printed page alone. Then one writes *over* the words in that magazine or book, using as a writing instrument a fibertip pen or similar instrument that makes a broad-stroke, transparent colored line. One can read what one has written as well as what one has written over. I know an ambitious physicist who buys paperback books by historic figures in physics and writes memoranda over those works as an aid in maintaining the feeling of irreverence that may go along with creative work. It is like a poem of Richard Wilbur, that tells of Degas' using a painting by El Greco to hang his pants on while he slept.

6

Traditional knowledge of creative thought

*Right so came by him Merlin like a child of fourteen
year of age, and saluted the king, and asked him why he
was so pensive. I may well be pensive said the king,
for I have seen the marvellest sight that ever I saw.
That know I well, said Merlin, as well as thyself, and of
all thy thoughts, but thou art but but a fool to take thought,
for it will not amend thee.*
LE MORTE D'ARTHUR, BOOK I, CHAPTER XX

Now the wondrous buzz and clatter of naturally occurring thought upon creative matters is taken up. At the end we find that the wonder of it all is coupled with the passivity of it all. Here, then, is the way the ancients, many of whom are alive and well today, did it.

Graham Wallas wrote a book called *The Art of Thought* (Wallas, 1926), which is cited everywhere but that few have given evidence of having read. It is true, as everyone who mentions the book reports, that Wallas broke the time-course of problem-solving into four stages: preparation, incubation, illumination, and verification. But Wallas was a teacher of political science by trade, an early member of the Fabian Society, and an author full of wit and wisdom. One sees him smile sweetly as he quotes T. H. Huxley, comparing the methods of Darwin with those of a "miraculous dog." One notes the bitterness of his smile as he accuses William James of missing the importance of his own analysis of *insight* because he was "strongly desirous of retaining certain opinions" (p. 212). And when he ends his book with the saddest passage of all, we see him weep hopefully. Having remarked that the place of consciousness in the universe will be sufficiently respected some day, and then experiments will be performed which are demanded by following reason, wherever she may take us, he closes by writing that in the meantime "whatever may prove to be the best art of thought will continue to be the best, whether many of those who have the necessary powers are enabled to practice it or few."

Were it possible—and Wallas does not for a moment doubt it—to bring conscious effort to bear to break the bumbling association-processes of ordinary thought in the interests of creative thinking, *where* is one to do it? Where in the presumed train of association ought one to break in? He gives up on any but a time-analysis, assuming that in *all* cases there are four stages, successive ones, in the making of a thought-achievement. There is preparation, when you fill up with information; incubation, when the *hidden work* is done out of sight of the mind's eye; illumination, when the *new* thought comes out into view; and verification, when the new thought is evaluated by the conscious gatekeepers, to the land where happy ideas turn into useful servants of mankind or into objects of aesthetic delight, or whatever else happens to ideas that *make it!*

Aristotle made a happy distinction between two kinds of knowledge: one needed by a pupil for him to equal his teacher; the other needed by a pupil for useful discussion to begin at all. The Wallas time-course has tended to be accepted as very basic knowledge. Indeed, we grant the need for preparation when some knowledge must be gained of what is already known, of incubation when time passes with uneasy emptiness, illumination when a solution to the difficulties experienced in incubation is offered in consciousness, and verification when the solution is tested out against prior knowledge and the search is made for new knowledge in accordance with relatively straightforward rules of procedure.

Beveridge (1957) discussed the stage of preparation in a noteworthy manner. Throughout his book he strains to bare both horns of each dilemma. He balances the advice to make a detailed study of the literature dealing with the problem of interest with Shaw's quip that "reading rots the mind." The sense in which Shaw was entirely correct is related to the incorporation of unsuccessful attacks upon the problem along with information concerning details of the problem. He counsels reading critically, as did Polya (1957), whose advice is to believe nothing, and to doubt only what is worth doubting. Many developing creative children meet discomfort and discouragement in education that stresses close attention to detailed facts, testing on trees students who want to comprehend forests.

Yet, some balance between learning what is already known and remaining aloof from traditional "errors" seems necessary to all serious commentators on this issue. It is impossible to find many examples of "good ideas," *qua* illumination, arising and being recognized without prior knowledge, *qua* preparation.

There are forms as well as content to be learned in preparation. The more varied successful problem-solving experiences one has had, the greater the chances of trying a variety of attacks on a problem. It is not that when one fails he can try, try again—it is that he can try *different* things. As we will see, and learn to regret deeply, the natural tendency is to keep trying the same old thing when illumination requires more flexibility than that.

Another sense in which preparation can hurt, henceforth, is the rather frequent case of having one's own early successes like an albatross on one's neck. We are amused today by the trouble that Charles Wheatstone was saddled with in 1852 when he thrashed about trying to surmount the easy success of his 1838 paper in which he had invented the stereoscope. Look, he had said, in 1838, Leonardo *et al.* really goofed in thinking that seeing real depth in pictures was impossible. For the eyes are separated by about three inches, one to the left of the other. Hence they get views from slightly different standpoints. So let us draw pictures with geometrical accuracy, one from a standpoint three inches to the left of the other, and let us view the one drawn from the left with the left eye while viewing the one drawn from the right with the right eye. Observe! Depth! And why? Because we have taken what *nature* made and *simulated nature exactly*. Each eye separately gets its own flat view of the world; together they make depth. Why? He did not know, but said that at least all previous thoughts on the matter had left out the remarkable power of the three-inch separation of the eyes and so were too restricted to be true.

Swiftly the industry of making handheld stereoscopes developed, the new technique of photography was rushed to development, and stereoscopic photographs of all the wonders of the world were taken, one a little to the left of the other. They were then bought by Victorian papas to pass around on winter's evenings. Never had a scientific article been so modestly written on so earthshaking a topic (it did not take much to shake Great Britain in those days). And never had it such an army of well-wishers behind it, pushing. Oliver Wendell Holmes, for instance, who himself invented one version of the handheld stereoscope, wrote in the *Atlantic Monthly* that the destruction of the

Pantheon would be no great loss since now one could see it again, depth included, by viewing stereograms of it (Holmes, 1861).

How poor Charles Wheatstone suffered from his success! His peaceful years inventing musical instruments and the like were buried in the clash of notoriety. The Wheatstone Bridge, which was invented by a man named Christie, came to be named after him, the most shy of men, a miraculous mouse thrust into the limelight. He would be on the program to deliver a speech, but would prevail upon a friend to deliver it for him, as he fled in fear. It was after such an incident at the Royal Institution, so tradition says, that the practice was begun there of locking the speaker in an anteroom under guard a half hour before the scheduled talk. We are told that this practice is in the interest of insuring a quiet period for the speaker to collect his thoughts free from possible intruders (Bragg, 1966). There was another need for that in those days.

Well, in 1852 Wheatstone struck again, writing a second paper on the stereoscope, but this time trying to renege on simulating Nature's way, instead *experimenting* with the stereoscope on what *never* occurs in nature. While his painful efforts seem now small mouse steps born of discomfort with what he had wrought (being aware that stereoscopy was too subject to reverent awe), his credo quoted as follows applies all the more to thought than it does to sensation.

To advance this inquiry beyond the point to which it has hitherto been brought, it is not sufficient to content ourselves with drawing conclusions from observations on the circumstances under which vision naturally occurs, as preceding writers on this subject mostly have done, but it is necessary to have more extended recourse to the methods so successfully employed in experimental philosophy, and to endeavor whenever it be possible, not only to analyse the elements of vision, but also to recombine them in unusual manners, so that they may be associated under circumstances that never naturally occur (Wheatstone, 1852).

Wallas was a member of the London School Board at a time when the issue of compulsory education up to the advanced age of 16 was being hotly debated.

In these more advanced times, children in school do face a rather grim problem. Einstein once wrote that it is a miracle that modern educational methods have not already strangled inquiry—for once started, inquiry's only need is freedom. "I believe that one could even deprive a healthy beast of prey of its voraciousness, if one could force it with a whip to eat continuously whether it were hungry or not" (*in* Klein, 1965). Indeed, there is more and more knowledge to be taken in. Even so, children are always "discovering" things about the world. But these discoveries are rediscoveries of old knowledge. Presumably the later realization that many of one's earlier discoveries were "old hat" does no harm. While it might lead a child to gobble up knowledge as a hedge against the disappointment of being late in his discoveries, this does not always happen. Just as creative research scientists tend to select themselves by finding their way to working as they want to, some children turn the traditional curriculum into the "creative" one by themselves—but at great hazard. The relation between creativity and intelligence in respect to personality patterns and school achievement is given serious study by Wallach and Kogan (1965). We may all know of students who refuse to learn certain topics at certain times—and such stories as Einstein's "unteachableness" are well known. To the extent that novel solutions are inhibited by knowledge of prior methods of attack, learning the facts and methods developed in one area can be preparation for work in another area. Beveridge gives several examples of men trained in one area solving problems in another area, and he attributes their success in part to their freedom from knowledge that inhibits solutions.

But how is it that knowledge can inhibit solutions? What in fact is the detailed relationship between preparation and illumination? Consider the first question, the relation between knowledge and solution. Surely there is a set of problems the solution to which is rather easy, given popular knowledge, e.g., simple arithmetic problems. And surely there is a set of problems the solution to which is rather easy, given more specialized knowledge, e.g., simple qualitative analysis in chemistry. And surely there is a class of problems the solution to which would be rather easy, given knowledge that is not available—e.g., simple qualitative analysis in chemistry prior to knowledge of how to make such analysis. It seems possible that all problems fall into one or another of these three classes. It is the third class that seems to be the most interesting; the solutions which occur here stand some chance of being called "discoveries," the most appealing ones being of the sort in which the knowledge needed for a rather easy solution is itself nowhere available. In this interesting class of problems, prior knowledge seems most likely to interfere in the solution. Certainly the easiest maze may be the one with the fewest wrong paths available. And useless knowledge may be seductive, distracting one from alternative efforts of greater value.

Given preparation, consider the relation between it and illumination. For the three classes of problems already described, illumination is the importation of that knowledge into the problem which makes the solution rather easy (and verification is the rather easy working out of the implications of the "good idea" and assessing the viability of it upon close study). The "good idea" is the confrontation of the problem by the knowledge that makes a solution rather easy. The "good idea" is a verbalization of what now must be verified; it springs from importing the appropriate knowledge into the problem. In rather prosaic instances, it may take the form, "Oh, now I see that *that* information is really relevant." In less prosaic cases, it may take the form, "Oh, *that* knowledge might solve the problem; I wonder if that knowledge can be attained." And "incubation," standing between preparation and illumination, is that period of time before one can make such a verbalization.

One man feels like the model for Rodin's "Le Penseur" during incubation, sitting silently ready to grab illumination as she comes by; but men of different temperaments are led to different activities *in media res*. Russell goes about his business thinking of other things; Helmholtz puts on his walking shoes and climbs a mountain; Wallas falls into the easy mindless occupation of doing dull administrative duties, and has a secret laugh. For he knows that both strenuous exercise and mindless busy work are less destructive to creative thinking-in-the-wild than a thing that neither the athlete nor the administrator has the time to fall into—namely, the habit of industrious passive reading.

Wallas quotes Schopenhauer, saying that to put down one's own thoughts to take up a book is a sin against the Holy Ghost; he also quotes Carlyle as telling Anthony Trollope that a man when traveling should not read, but should sit still and label his thoughts.

It is the passivity of the reading that lulls the mind that Wallas most objects to; and we will have to admit that past some preparation on a problem one might be better for not reading anything at all.

The black, aching paralysis of problem-appropriate action that is characteristic of the incubation stage of problem solving is a painting on the large canvas of expanded time, the picture of the "confused, dazed, scatterbrained state" that often comes upon us unbidden.

Most people probably fall several times a day onto a fit of something like this: the eyes are fixed on vacancy, the sounds of the world melt into confused unity, the attention is dispersed so that the whole body is felt, as it were, at once, and the foreground of consciousness is filled, if by anything, by a sort of solemn surrender to the empty passing of time. In the dim background of our mind we know meanwhile what we ought to be doing: getting up, dressing ourselves, answering the person who has spoken to us, trying to make the next step in our reasoning. But somehow we cannot *start*; the *pensée de derrière la tête* fails to pierce the shell of lethargy that wraps our state about. Every moment we expect the spell to break, for we know no reason why it should continue. But it does continue, pulse after pulse, and we float with it, until—also without reason that we can discover—an energy is given, something—we know not what—enables us to gather ourselves together, we wink our eyes, we shake our heads, the background-ideas become effective, and the wheels of life go round again (James, 1890, Vol. I, p. 402).

When overcome thus in problem-solving one does not take vigorous shots at trying out an assortment of potential solutions. To this state, the pressure of time is welcome, as is the spur of adversity. "Damn braces," Blake wrote, "bless relaxes."

Notable discoveries may give thanks which may be deserved to the cleverness of their discoverers in arranging for an alarm clock to shriek, awake! Among untold others, Edison and Pasteur are rumored to have shared the technique of selecting a problem to solve, becoming frozen in incubation, and informing the press that the solution had been made, and scheduling a press conference to announce it; then under the pressure of time that they had arranged for themselves, breaking out of deep freeze to illumination.

B. M. Kedrov (1966–67) reports, on the basis of finding papers belonging to Mendeleev, that the discovery of the periodic table was made under the conditions of acute time-pressure. Poor Mendeleev faced the problem of wanting to outline the next volume of the text-book on chemistry he was writing, and was puzzling over some reason this should follow that, rather than something else, presumably out of a wish to have some principle to order the elements to save him from the discomfort of each time deciding what to write about next. At breakfast he played around with pencil and paper, jotting down the elements and their atomic numbers in various arrangements, but realizing that he had to leave for a trip, he gave up filling paper with lists, slumped into the freeze of incubation, got out some cards to play a hand of patience, and "Oh!"—he saw it was quick and easy to arrange playing cards on the desk, wrote the elements one to a playing card, fooled around a while, and there was a good order of the elements. Everything else then followed rather smoothly. Kedrov gives some credit to *Zeitnöt* (a term meaning the pressure of time, used to describe the condition of a chess player when he must decide the next several moves in too short a time), but indeed there is no evidence that time or anything else at all—anger, pleasure, cloudbursts, or uncinate fits— is the sure sign of the end of incubation.

Illumination, the end of incubation, the breaking of the freeze, the turning round again the wheels of life in regard to action on the problem, may be presaged by intimation. Wallas says: "that moment in the Illumination phase when our fringe-consciousness of an association-train is in the state of rising consciousness which indicates that the fully conscious flash of success is coming." The question that has often led men to speak without thinking too much is how the illumination comes about in spontaneous problem-solving. The problem may be in awareness, but no knowledge is seen as allowing a rather easy solution.

How is that knowledge found? How does incubation give way to illumination? Traditionally, it has been said that unconscious shufflings and reshufflings of ways of stating the problem and importations of pieces of knowledge occur, and such examples as Poincaré's "insight" while alighting from a bus are typical. One is told to allow unconscious work to occur; Rudyard Kipling, in discussing the presentation of "good ideas" to him unbidden, gave the advice: "Drift, wait, and obey." One goal of a study of heuristics is to design a less passive alternative.

Both Woodworth (1953) and Usher (1954) pooh-pooh the importa-tion into the game of the idea of unconscious mental activity during incubation. In its place, Woodworth supposes that conscious mental activity has sufficient time (and is really relevant) to the transformation of incubation to insight—or, in the Wallas terminology, illumination. After all, says Woodworth, perhaps there is a short period of intense concentration on the problem as incubation ends—and, anyway, the problem does "consciously recur" now and then during incubation.

With the best will in the world, solution fails us sometimes. Woodworth (1938, p. 823) took a serious look at what previous failure to solve some problem looked like to the problem-solver *after* he solved it. The result might be important in the design of problem-solution heuristics. The usual report was that the trouble had been that one assumed, in some more or less vague way, that a more complicated solution would be necessary.

Abbott Payton Usher (1954) denies that the solution to some problem smoothly follows from some way of looking at the problem, for we cannot know the things we have failed to accomplish, the discoveries that for whatever reason remain unborn. There are resistances, Usher writes, that stand in the path of certain men at certain times coming to certain solutions. Perhaps that is true. But it is uncontestedly true that when 'tis done 'tis seen as easy, before 'tis done 'tis seen as *anything but* easy.

As you look around you at discoveries you might have made but didn't—frozen food, say, or holograms—and if you find your way to understanding the basis of these techniques and see how awfully simple it is, at bottom, you can probably agree with Woodworth, and all others who have seen the issue of problem-solving backwards, that easy solutions are early seen as too simple to work, that something more complicated must be necessary.

Richard Feynman (1965, p. 171) surveys this issue from the heady standpoint of theoretical physics rather than theoretical psychology. The mark of truth as one guesses at a formula, he remarks, is that the good guess has beauty and simplicity, and that more comes out than goes in as one computes the consequences of the guess. When crackpots make simple guesses, it is easy to see that they are mistaken; but an inexperienced student makes a complicated guess, "But I know it is not true because the truth always turns out to be simpler than you thought."

Consider the *verbalization* of the illumination. The emotional pang of intimation is almost entirely an emotional call that "something is here!" And then, *almost immediately*, that which is here is given to awareness. But not quite all at once. There are laboratory journals in which full record is made as an aid to memory. Commonly this pattern of laboratory journal entries occurs. An entry as some topic or other is made and dated (with the time of day and the date of the entry). Then an illumination occurs. "Oh! The . . . ." And then the time and date of that entry. It may happen that the entry totals 10 or 12 words. It indeed seemed "a flash of insight." Yet the time it took to write those 10 or 12 words may be 15 minutes. What, then, is presented whole to awareness? I think it may only be the "Oh! something is *there*" and the relatively long time between the "oh!" and the end of the entry is taken up by a very active conscious effort to make some adequate verbalization. Perhaps the shufflings and reshufflings of possibilities occur *after* the "oh!" So the possibility is this: The first intimation of an illumination is an experience of "Oh! There's something now," and then "time seems to stand still" while there is conscious arranging of the "pieces of the puzzle" that is then seen as a "good idea." The "oh!" may be a sign that the problem is solved (as the traditional view would suppose) *or* a sign that now it *can* be solved with a bit of conscious work! The value of considering the latter possibility is that if the "oh!" merely allows, and the "oh!" is merely an emotional state in which heightened problem-solving play can occur, it might fall out that the "oh!" state of emotion is controllable; that there is a controllable emotional state of heightened cognitive ability.

This hopeful suggestion is always met with an interesting absence of enthusiasm; perhaps, like most complicated suggestions, it seems too complicated to be true.

Einstein wrote that at one period he became aware of the general direction in which a solution lay, and while some years passed before illumination, the period of incubation was not empty: the general form of the solution was fairly clear. This state of mind is similar to the state of mind in which one tries to remember a forgotten name. We may all have had the experience of forgetting a name, say the name of one's second-grade teacher. One may remember her appearance and her manner and some particular incidents in which she was involved, but her name is lost. Yet, one "knows" the general form of her name. One can usually say, for instance, "No, it wasn't Smith, or Jones, or Miller, or Roberson; it was more like Anthony, or Cagny, or Monohan, or Reilly." And later, "It was an Irish name. Oh, it was O'Shay." Throughout the search for the lost name, one can reject names that were not the correct one even though the correct one escapes capture. Furthermore, one could pick the lost name from a list in which it was embedded, if only one were given such a list. An intriguing possibility is this: When the stage has been reached in which one can verbalize some features of a solution—i.e., the solution lies "at the tip of one's tongue" —the solution has already been made (as a lost name was once learned); the problem now is to release it from cognitive inhibition. It seems possible to design research on this matter when it is looked at in this way—for example, perhaps any technique for reducing cognitive rigidity would be useful. Certainly the old advice, "take counsel of your pillow," seems consistent with this view. And it is very passive indeed.

We have watched the process of spontaneous creative thought as it muddles along, perhaps not only in the most but also in the least important acts of problem-solving. It is a passive pasttime, for the most part—meaning that no one knows the rules of doing it. There are individual differences in "talent" that make all the difference.

There is a parable about long division that is too good to be true. Once upon a time the algorithm for long division had not been worked out and made public, but in that day there were a few men who now and then came up with the right answer to a long division problem. The universities snatched them up and gave them advanced degrees on the spot, and their brilliance and creativity were widely proclaimed. But now the algorithm is taught to children. There has been a timid suspicion on this planet for hundreds of years that there may be algorithms for all heavy things, and we can see the ancients inching toward them, toward algorithms.

Ramon Lull was born about 1232 in Majorca and died in 1315 at the hands of a Saracen mob he was exhorting to convert to Christianity. During his life he wrote more than enough to give birth to a cult that survived more than five centuries. And he was to give in his life and work a figure of *farfelu* which inspired Rabelais, Francis Bacon, and Jonathan Swift. Rabelais wrote in *Pantagruel*, Chapter 6, "Laisse-moi l'astrologie divinatrice et l'art Lullius, comme abus et vanités." Francis Bacon said of Lull's *Ars Magna*, "methodus imposturae, quae tamen quibusdam ardelionibus acceptissima procul dubio fuerit," and Swift put Gulliver at the miraculous automatic book-writing machine of Lagado, a device of Lullian temper and one that Lull must have used himself if he is to be credited with writing all the books he is said to have authored.

After an early manhood of amorous adventure in what we are led to believe were the boyish high spirits of the Middle Ages, he abandoned his wife and small children and at age 40 published a several-volume religious work of about one million words in length. Having served his apprenticeship at unwilling women's skirts and at profligate authorship, he set out to convert the heathens. In his books that treat the problem of conversion, the heathens are very reasonable chaps indeed. No mere hitting them on the head would do at all. What was needed was sheer convincing.

Look back now seven centuries to a time of high spirits when the troubador destined to author the *Ars Magna* rode after an attractive, unwilling woman into church, still on his horse, only to be hooted from the hall by congregants half amused and half outraged. Follow him up Mount Randa to a Majorcan cave where he awaited divine inspiration. Follow him as he wrote *Ars Magna*, and the hundreds of books later on. He tried to compensate for the fall of *Ars Magna* dead-born from his pen, repeating his algorithm again and again and again, each time changing a little, and each time managing to compose some pretty classy prose. His English-language translator and biographer of 1929 (Peers, 1929) wrote a 400-page book about Ramon Lull, devoting about 399 pages of it to Lull the lover, Lull the churchman, Lull the writer, and Lull the legend, and about one page to the *Ars Magna*. Lull's obsession was with a great and general art of invention and conversion of heathens through his method's particular kind of perfection.

That particular kind of perfection is the awful error of the Middle Ages of assuming that all the important facts are in, the votes counted, and Truth elected along with a set of inexorable laws of nonempirical logical necessity. Lull's dreadful mistake was solving the problem of always being right. The method involves semimechanical syllogizing through the use of a prototype of the later-to-be-invented circular sliderule (Lull lived centuries before Napier). "Those who give themselves to such studies as these with assiduity," says Lull, "will find themselves constructing syllogisms almost without knowing it, even in their sleep" (Peers, p. 155).

Yet, Lull had his talent at scoring in literature, before European literature had been born; he comes two centuries before Rabelais and Malory, and a century before Chaucer, though he was a contemporary of Roger Bacon and of Dante, Boccaccio, and Petrarch. "Say, O Fool! What meanest thou by a marvel?" He answered, "It is a marvel to love things absent more than things present, and to love things visible and things corruptible more than things invisible and incorruptible." This from *Book of the Lover and the Beloved* (Peers, p. 189).

A favorite Lull story concerns the 1306 lecture by Duns Scotus, then a young firebrand, sent from Oxford to teach at the Sorbonne, where one day the old bearded Lull sat grimacing with disagreement, perhaps absent-mindedly. In a huff, the young teacher asked a question designed to show up the ignorance of the silly old goat.

Duns Scotus: *"Dominus, quae pars?"* (What part of speech is Lord?)
Lull: *"Dominus non est pars, sed totum."* (The Lord is not a part, but the whole.) The Lullian legend goes that Ramon then embarked on a spontaneous fiery lecture on the perfection of the Divine Nature, and then quickly wrote a book entitled *Dominus Quae Pars? concerning the debate of Ramon with Scotus.*

By the time of Peers, none of Lull's inventive art was taken seriously, but his life and legend as a religious figure was. At the present day, it is Martin Gardner who rescued Lull from libraries in departments of divinity and brought him to attention as a rather wrong-headed precursor of computers (Gardner, 1968). Gardner described Lull's fantastic circles within circles, with terms written on their circumferences, for the purpose of juxtaposing terms of interest for the conversion of heathens (e.g. Truth, Glory, Greatness, Length, Potency, Wisdom, Virtue, and Goodness). Exhausting allowable combinations is easy by using Lull's wheels, and perhaps useful in discovery. "What is invention, after all, except the knack of finding new and useful combinations of old principles?" Gardner asks (p. 20). He suggests that it is easy to get close to a Lullian frame of mind by building some nested circles moveable separately, with terms of interest to you, then playing at twisting the wheels and letting the mind dwell on the strange, and perhaps portentous, combinations that show up.

We have not done with Lull as yet, for he will be put to work by Ogden soon, not for the purpose of grinding out true statements, but for the purpose of grinding out grammatical statements.

Wallas (1926, p. 28) supposed that successive creative thinkers learned something from their predecessors, that there was something Plato learned from Socrates, Sophocles from Aeschylus, Faraday from Davy, and Marlowe, Jonson, and Shakespeare from each other; something which "changed his use of his mind and helped to give efficiency to his thought."

Some have supposed that there is a set of forms, or tactics, or "cognitive moves" that crop up in solution after solution—that there might indeed be a set of solutions that is finite, so that they could easily be tailored to fit any problem that happened to walk in the door to the shop.

Of course, the problem that arises is how to compile such a list. Some busy archivist could perhaps while away some rainy days going through the history of discovery and invention with an attitude like naturalistic observation but with a goal of botanization: putting different solutions in different piles, similar solutions in the same pile. Should it be that the set of all solutions is finite and could be found this way, new problems would try on old solutions till one is found that fits.

To simplify any complex system, one can attempt to analyze it into a small set of elements which recur in lawful combinations. At the edge of plausibility this "cognitive move" often slurs over distinctions that have a good deal of force from some other point of view. One common example concerns numerous efforts to shoot all of biology through with a few arrangements of elements, whereby the distinction between plant life and animal life is slurred over. At the turn of the last century, for example, Loeb noticed that the tropisms of animals are the same thing as the tropisms of plants, except that the time between stimulus and movement is much greater in plants than animals. More recently, biochemical research has capitalized heavily on ignoring differences between plants and animals with respect to the organic compounds they contain (Szent-Gyorgyi, 1963) and by the turn of the next century there may exist leisurely articles on the psychoanalysis of grass.

One example of how a set of cognitive moves might be found shows how very arbitrary and unpleasant the task becomes. Skip through a volume of the *Encyclopaedia Britannica* and come upon something that seems to be hilariously clever. The general Cyrus had faced the problem of getting his army across the Gyndes, and solved it by digging a channel to divert the river so that his army could march forward dry shod. Centuries later, Faraday faced the problem of getting a wire to rotate in the electrical field of a rotating magnet in order to bring the electric motor and generator into being. He arranged to divert the current in the place where it canceled the effects upon the wire. "Divert the barrier to move ahead," one might say to oneself. But look at the arbitrariness of that way of saying it and recoil.

Yet, one man chose to sweat it out. Zuce Kogan (1956) wrote a book about a little set of ready-made solutions to fit needy practical problems. He refrained from any claim that his small set was exhaustive. His approaches include one that advises removing something when it is unnecessary and troublesome, but whether that can be considered as being equivalent to advising diverting the barrier to move ahead is a question that boggles one's mind. Nonetheless, there are times when one cannot encourage oneself too much, though I despair at the arbitrariness of Kogan's method. One needs to *exhaust* the possibilities which never had been done by this sort of botanizing in this overgrown field.

The mathematician has sometimes had a better time of it than anyone else in grappling with discovery, for the moves to make in mathematics are ones that are explicitly taught and the solution of a rather hard mathematical problem takes no longer than the writing of a poem. Poets are jolly companions, as Kurt Vonnegut once wrote, because they are always between jobs, while novelists are no good to have at conferences, for all they can do as they pass each other is to groan like great wounded bears. There are practical problems and scientific problems that take a century or so to solve. It can all be speeded up in the games that mathematicians play. Perhaps for that reason, great mathematicians have turned to the study of heuristics more often than have men who are more like novelists, taking months to write a paper, years chewing away at an enticing lead, feeling like one of those bears. Polya (1957) reviewed the work of several mathematicians interested in heuristics in the context of a book that expanded on a set of questions to ask oneself when confronted with a mathematical problem, questions that are designed to propel the problemsolver out of incubation's freeze into the warmth of heady action.

Among men who fiddled with the problem in the mathematical tradition leading to Polya were Pappus, Descartes, Leibnitz, and Bolzano (Polya, 1957, p. 112). The aim of heuristics is "to study the methods and rules of discovery and invention," wrote Polya, noting that heuristics was as good as forgotten. He wrote the book which brought it back to life.

Polya presented a set of questions to ask oneself when working on a problem (e.g., "What is the unknown? Do you know a related problem? Did you use the whole condition?") and developed the idea of *plausible reasoning*.

For example, suppose a general conjecture A implies a particular consequent, B. If it is found that B is false, it is concluded that A is false, by a familiar pattern of demonstrative reasoning. But suppose B is true. Then there is no demonstrated conclusion about A, for the verification of a consequent does not prove the conjecture. But, A is more credible when B is found to be true, a pattern of plausible inference Polya calls "the fundamental inductive pattern" (Polya, 1954, vol. II, p. 4).

So maybe the awful truth is that thoughts do not change much, but the same old thoughts go round and round. This seems particularly obvious as one sets out to solve some problem. One goes round and round, returning to where one began, like a traveler in a maze. The problem-solver has always supposed that there is an art to thought. When successful, he felt he was close upon it and when failing, he felt it was well out of reach. But perhaps those opinions have nothing to do with the bones of the matter.

To progress, given a barrier, the strong find a way to go over it while the lazy find a way to go round it. Then how can we make progress? Well, what is the nature of the barrier that blocks progress? The nature of the barrier in thought has been taken to be functional fixedness—the habitual attack upon some problem which when it fails is still used. What can give variety to the set of attacks on a problem?

Of all the possible ways to attack the general problem of how to get past barriers to the advancement of thought, the most common is the most perverse—to study how to build barriers to thought. This dilemma ought to remind clinical psychologists of other cases of "identification with the aggressor." It is, however, a strategy in research in psychology with a very long history.

When William McDougall left Harvard in favor of Duke, he swept down the east coast expecting to gather up a faculty for the new Department of Psychology. One of those he gathered in was young Karl Zener, who worked with Karl Duncker in Berlin in 1927 in studying methods to block the advance of thought.

The work was later carried forward at rather a lively pace, principally by Abraham Luchins. His are the well-known water-jar problems (Luchins, 1942). See also Golann (1963).

The water-jar problems show that it is rather easy to form a simple habit in the attack upon a set of problems—and then to become a slave to that habit, doing things thereon in the old-way-that-has-worked. It is lovely to do things in a routine way, without having each time to decide how to do it. Very general methods are especially good, for their field of application is so very wide. Luchins' problems show that people prefer old habits—even very arbitrary ones—to new gropings. Of course, the analysis of such a thing as this need not be entirely soporific. Maybe all that is wrong is that one falls into the *wrong* routine and does not have a ladder to climb out.

7
Recurrence and creation

*It is as irrelevant how you came to that idea as whether
you came to this room by the elevator or by the stairs.*
KARL ZENER

We are now well acquainted with the idea that consciousness has
the features of a plenum; that it may be entirely full of its contents,
whatever they are: and, therefore, that all movement in consciousness
may be cyclic. On this basis the recurrence of thoughts and actions is
just what we might expect. We are now acquainted with the idea that
there is something called creative thinking and problem-solving about
which nothing is so clear as that it is a chancy passive pursuit.

Finally, we are acquainted with some thrashings of the awakening
beast, some rousing from the long sleep of thought, some attempts to
jab it, poke it, mechanize it, shatter it, reform it, and shake it awake—
so that we might find a way to do the same things we do passively, as
in dreaming, while we are awake and with all our wits about us.

We have seen that memory is aided by an externalized similacrum
of the hidden plenum, and that a little intellectual progress can be
made in taking words and separating them into a pile called content
and a pile called form.

We will now find that the little heap of words that sits in the pile
called form determines the structure of action and of everything new.
We organize this section around an article by Duncker. This is in
tribute to Karl Zener, my teacher, who had worked with Duncker
on these matters. My misfortune is that while Zener still lived I did
not know of this connection.

Theories early in the day are just speculations about some domain.
This has been true for creative problem-solving. At other times, theories
are models. Generally speaking, a good model is a trifle more than a
good metaphor or a good analogy. A good model allows bringing the
domain and the model into a comparable scale, so that predictions of
magnitudes can be made. This has not yet been at all typical of theories
of creative problem-solving. At yet another time, theories bite to the

bone of the matter, picking out the simple structure of a domain. Karl Duncker came to such a profound analysis of the domain of creative problem-solving, and it will be wise to take him more literally and seriously than he took his own work. It is a great irony in the history of psychology that he had a solution to his problem within his grasp, but became functionally fixated on his concept of functional fixedness, a complication that blocked his insight into the simple statement of the solution to his problem.

Duncker introduced his monograph with a paragraph that follows:

A problem arises when a living creature has a goal but does not know how this goal is to be reached. Whenever one cannot go from the given situation to the desired situation simply by action, then there is recourse to thinking. . . . Such thinking has the task of devising some action which may mediate between the existing and desired situations. Thus the solution of a "practical" problem must fulfill two demands: in the first place its realization must bring about the goal situation, and in the second place one must be able to arrive at it from the given situation simply through action.

When a practical problem is solved by chance *qua* trial and error it is solved through action which mediates between the given and desired situations. When a practical problem is solved by "insight," there must also be action which mediates between the given and desired situations. Action solves problems—it is the immediate cause of the arrival at the desired situation. Thought or chance may be a remote cause. *The theoretical point is this: the basic feature of all possible solutions to a problem is that set of all possible actions that might mediate between the given and the desired solution.* We can make the set of *allowable* actions as large or as small as we like in experiments on problem-solving, and we can allow subjects to work on problems on their own, or we can help or hinder them in various ways from finding some action that mediates between the given and the desired situation. Much of the work that has been done from Duncker's day to this one has concerned itself with functional fixedness, which in the context of Duncker's first paragraph defines a spasticity of intent, a blockage of possible action.

If we knew the set of all possible actions, we would, by Duncker's analysis, be in the position of simplifying the problem of creative problem-solving. In the solution of any particular problem, we must select out of the set of all possible actions a *particular* action. Let us begin by doing a thought-experiment. Imagine two creatures, one very simple and the other very complex. For the former, only simple actions are allowed; for the latter, the most complex actions that are imaginable. Put both creatures in the shape of a human being. What can one do that the other cannot?

For the first case, take someone who is paralyzed to the extent of only being able to blink his eyes. For the second kind, imagine a prima ballerina. The ballerina can blink her eyes *and* do other things, too, in a sequence of great complexity. She can do more things with her body. But let us supply each with a Waldo, a robotlike device that performs actions with its own parts as it is led to do by the actions of its human operator. Let the Waldo for the paralyzed man be programmed to perform all its actions by the sequencing of its operator's eyeblinks, with the speed that the sequence is to be run off also coded. Give a similar device to the ballerina, to be controlled by her body movements, again with a code put in for tempo. Now watch the two robots. Both do the same things, modulated by differences in gracefulness perhaps in programming, but the same things.

Picture a bag of marbles with supernatural powers. What is the set of its *possible actions*? How are we to *describe* them?

Just as there must exist a set of all actions, no matter how easy or hard it might be to describe them, so must there be a set of all possible thoughts—again, no matter how easy or hard it might be to describe them. In the case of action, there are few people who assert that there are inchoate actions—even ballet has a written notation that directs dancers to the set of actions and the tempo of their execution. However, very few people suppose that all states of consciousness and all the contents in all the states can be formally described. Traditionally, it has been supposed that there are cognitions that can be described for the most part in words, actions that can also for the most part be described in words, but also feelings that words do not map. But great mimes do manage to map emotions with actions, and the actions themselves can be described in words.

The subset of all thoughts that is relevant to heuristics is the specific problem now. And now a serious decision has to be made: namely, that everything I write is to be written in the form of words. Thus the problem becomes the subset of all words. Which words?

We now must ring in Ogden, as he rang in Karl Pearson. In a rather pretentious passage of his "The Grammar of Science" Pearson made an invitation which Ogden later accepted:

A fundamental part of logic is the study of the right use of language, the clear definition and, if needful, invention of terms—*Orthology*. The object of the present *Grammar* has been chiefly to show how a want of clear definition has led to the metaphysical obscurities of modern science (Pearson, 1937).

Ogden made a giant step in orthology, finding a way to get rid of words.

Ogden invented a short-form of English in which, for a start, the needs of everyday life can be expressed. The beauty of the invention is that it consists entirely of a vocabulary. Just the full set of words that can be used. Taken from the larger set of all English words, the vocabulary is made up of 850 simple English words (Ogden, 1934).

Of those words, 16 are verbs (operations), and 20 are directions. Just about all the others are the names of qualities and things, words like "history," "rice," "strong," and "flower." As it happens, the vocabulary of Basic English, with skill in its use, results in a fine language of some power and great clarity.

Given the problem of specifying "cognitive moves"—à la Zuce Kogan and suchlike efforts—the vocabulary of Basic English forces simplicity on their statement. Given a set of "cognitive moves," however stated at the start, a translation of them into Basic English must have the effect of making them more comparable, one with another, as they are stuffed into a smaller universe. Particular words are necessarily transformed into more generally applicable ones. For after all is said and done, Basic does say everything that can be said and done.

Graham (1965) edited a scientific dictionary written all in the Basic English 850-word vocabulary.

How can we make Basic English fit Duncker's first paragraph? Can we describe an action in Basic English? Can we, in the extreme or "mad" case describe the set of all actions? Let the vocabulary of Basic English be the only words we use. Let us, then, consider the forms of sentences.

It is here that Ogden chose a maneuver in the style of Ramon Lull, describing the "word wheel," naming it the "panopticon"—"because all the necessary units are seen together." The word wheel in the specific simple form described by Ogden (1934, p. 305) consists of seven circles of increasing diameter piled on top of each other in order of decreasing diameter. In the smallest inner top circle are the words "will," "would," "may" and "might;" in the second ring are some verbs ("put," "take," "get," "give," "keep," "let," "have," "make," "come," "go"); in the third are 12 adjectives like "simple" and "some;" in the fourth are 20 nouns, like "sand" and "thing;" in the fifth are 20 directions, like "on" and "across;" in the sixth are 21 nouns, like "farm" and "edge;" in the seventh are 10 adverbs and connectives, like "here" and "but." By agreeing to put "a" or "the" where needed and starting the sentence with the word "I," one can get many mechanically produced sentences as one turns each of the wheels independently of each of the others. The sentences are grammatical. For example, "I may take some sand across the edge here" and "I might keep a simple thing across the farm, but [recycling] I would have some sand on the edge here."

Perhaps Ogden knew about Lull—but the idea of a wheel is as old as chariots, so it should be no surprise to find it coming along here and there. Recall that Lull used it to make syllogisms—statements that had the look of unarguable Truth. Ogden used to to make grammatical sentences that had the look of hidden Thought. Strip the frills from the panopticon and one has the "heuropticon," a wheel-thing that has the look of heuristic Action.

We have already quoted Gardner (as he talked about Lull) as saying what has been said uncountable times before: that all there is to discovery and invention is putting a couple of old things in a new relation. An Ogden word-wheel that is stripped for action does it, *exhausting the possibilities* that can be stated in Basic English. The elementary form of a statement of an action is "taking one thing in some relation to another thing." The same elementary sentence is the form of a sentence to describe the statement of a discovery, an invention, or, indeed, an idea. The "things" can be anything you like, as multiple as the things of the world can be, but the relations are small in number, in point of fact, if the elementary form of an action-sentence is "Take one thing dash another thing," there are only 42 words in the set of all Basic English words that can by the wildest stretch of imagination fit where the dash is. The words follow (from Crovitz, 1967).

about	at	for	of	round	to
across	because	from	off	still	under
after	before	if	on	so	up
against	between	in	opposite	then	when
among	but	near	or	though	where
and	by	not	out	through	while
as	down	now	over	till	with

An old experiment in the psychology of problem-solving is important now. It is the *Umweg* problem. Put some corn on the ground. Put a transparent barrier, like a sheet of glass, in front of the corn. Put a hungry chicken in front of the glass. The barrier is between the chicken and the corn. The chicken acts in a very stupid manner. It tries to get through the barrier that it cannot get through, to go to the corn which it cannot go to, but rather must go away from to go round the barrier to get to the corn. The chicken is wearing a relational-filter before its mind's eye; all it will act on is going straight *to* the corn.

Somebody described an analogous situation. There is a very long line of traffic in the turn-left lane of a highway, but none in the straight-through right lane. Drivers, however, wear their turn-left filters before their mind's eye, seldom doing the "creative, intelligent" thing of going straight across, then going round the block, thence wheeling down the road before any of those twenty cars ahead have got past the stoplight.

Success in problem-solving comes from changing the relational-filter before the mind's eye, tacitly rippling through the set of actions that are possible, and then having the wit to recognize a solution when you see one. Or, if you are very stupid but very quick, like a computer, trying *all* the possible actions till the goal is attained and it is time to stop.

This computer maneuver has been simulated by busy inventive men whose biographers have found their methods out. Perhaps the most instructive case has to do with building a working model of the system you want to change, and then tinkering with it. Tinkering with a model of the thing is harmless; in an undisciplined run through the possible actions you may be lucky enough to come upon a solution. Thomas Edison was a great one for tinkering with models of things, and might be a pattern on which to build a discoverer-computer.

Edison himself was no slowpoke. The glory of his youth was that he had a fast, legible hand, and was capable of writing at a rapid rate. But, according to a son, later on he had little power of abstraction, being always in need of seeing a thing in its concrete form, and tinkering with it. One of the problems that is described well by Josephson (1959, p. 123) is Edison's work on the quadraplex—his putative discovery of how to send four simultaneous messages along a telegraph wire, two in each direction at once. This was important at the time— it would quadruple the power of the telegraph without the need of having to build four times the number of wires. Edison built an "analog" of the electric wire, with pipes and valves and assorted gadgets for affecting the flow of the water in the pipe. Using the gadgets to force water back and forth, in the pattern of wires in the system that was planned, he tinkered and ended with separating the separable features of the flow of current, sending one message controlled by one, and another controlled by another (Josephson, p. 124).

Edison also had a workshop that does in space what notebooks do in time, allowing one project to infect a neighboring one, so that moves made here may also be tried out there. His lab was a big barn with worktables along the room holding separate projects in progress. He would inspect one, then another. Not a bad trick for an ancient to come upon for switching relational-filters. That and working a 20-hour day stood him in good stead indeed. Of course, by his lights he was a failure where inventions were concerned, for he never made any money from them except when he set up commercial ventures to control that practical part of things himself. Yet, when he visited Pasteur once, Edison did not make a very good impression, for Pasteur was horrified at glimpsing the distractions attached to Edison's commercial ventures.

Notice that the switching of relational-filters is hard for problem-solvers to do naturally. The relevant history of intellectual precursors of this small work are reviewed engagingly by Mandler and Mandler (1964), who covered in some detail a history of changing emphasis that evolved from analysis of raw consciousness to inquiries into problem-solving. They detected a growing tendency to probe the processes that intervene between problem and solution (p. 276). That review ends with Duncker.

Duncker studied this problem: to get rid of an inoperable stomach tumor without harming the healthy tissue of the body, by using rays that can be modulated in intensity; at a high enough intensity, they destroy. He gave a protocol, but not a good one. The experimenter kept butting in, giving hints, asking leading questions. Nonetheless, the remarks of the subject—his attempts to solve the problem aloud—are instructive when they are put into relational language. The sequence of comments, so translated, is this:

1. Take the rays *through* the esophagus.
2. Take the sensitivity *from* the tissues.
3. Take tissue *off* the tumor.
4. Take strong rays *after* weak rays.
5. Take a shield *on* stomach walls.
6. Take the tumor *across* the stomach.
7. Take a cannula *through* the stomach wall.
8. Take the power *from* the rays.
9. Take the tumor *to* the exterior.
10. Take strong rays *after* weak rays.
11. Take strong rays *after* weak rays.
12. Take the rays *from* the body, or take the power *from* the rays.
13. Take the tumor *at* the focus of rays.
14. Take one ray *across* another ray.

It is possible to devise an irreverent method for solving "practical" problems with the use of elementary sentences that list the *full* set of possible actions that that form of sentence can cover in the vocabulary of Basic English. That is the amusing task of the next chapter.

One thing that is wrong with the mind's eye is that it has relational-filters that get stuck. Let us speed up the exchange of filters.

With respect to the x-ray problem as given by Duncker, there are at least two domain-words, "ray" and "stomach-tumor." The Basic English translation of ray is "any of a number of straight lines going out in different directions from a common point." Stomach is "a bag-like expansion of the digestion-pipe." Tumor is "an abnormal mass from normal body materials." Thus the problem might become using lines to get rid of a mass in a bag. In this particular case, the translation into Basic English reduces the problem very quickly to a diagrammatic stark form of it.

I leave the playing of such a diagram to the reader, merely noting that, given a mass in a bag and given lines emanating from a point, there are

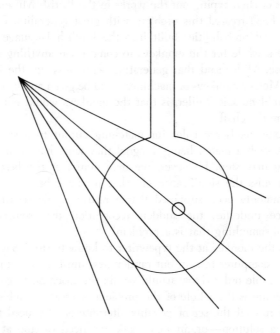

many possibilities other than framing the question of how to get rid of the mass, i.e., take the mass from the bag. There are words other than *from*.

We can learn a small but very important thing from some protocols we collected on the relational algorithm in Duncker's problems from college students, one of whom was poor Penelope (who had done so badly on her walk down Gorky Street).

A group of 10 undergraduates was given the x-ray problem and the single sentence, "Take one ray across another ray." Everybody quickly saw the solution. But not Penelope. She rejected the sentence, never having her mind's eye put the tumor at the *intersection* of the two rays. Alas. It is not automatic; success is not assured; there is no royal road nor indeed any commoner's road that is sure to lead to knowledge.

Given the "laws of probability," chances are that a bunch of monkeys at a bunch of typewriters would peck out nonsense, but take the extreme case of their typing out the works in the British Museum. Miller (1951, p. 809) treated this problem with great generality. Even given the sequential probabilities built into the English language, it would take quite a while for the monkeys to come upon anything that made much sense. Miller said that generating sense was *not* the interesting problem. Men or monkeys or machines could be given an algorithm to do it. The problem, said Miller, is that the monkeys would not know the wheat from the chaff.

What one needs are rules for matching output to a standard, the making of such a match being a signal that sense has been made and the typing may stop. However, we may note that the best of us do sometimes miss the significance of what we have before us—indeed, it has commonly been supposed that a rather mystic restructuring of significance underlies the sudden recognition that something is a solution to something that is a problem.

How is the monkey at the typewriter to know to stop? Say we chose to set up a computer to spin out randomness until it came to some, for us, recognizable order. How would we fix the machine to go and then stop? Stopping is the whole of the problem of creative problem-solving if we can run off the set of possible alternatives. We need the wit to recognize a solution—or, in plain talk, we need to stop at the right alternative. How is that to be arranged?

Suppose we know the goal. In the x-ray problem it is most easily stated in two parts: first, the tumor is destroyed; second, the tissue that is not the tumor is unaffected. The second part is always satisfied while the first part is simultaneously satisfied when the goal is transformed into this: tumor is in body; body is around the tumor. The goal is satisfied when we can reach the sentence: the tumor is destroyed; the body around it is unaffected. We draw a figure. On the line AB the energy is constant and too low to destroy tissue. On the line CD the energy is also constant and too low to destroy tissue. So at $a,b,c,$ and d—the body around the tumor—there is no effect. But at the crossing, the energy sums and whatever tissue is there is destroyed. Put the tumor there—the tumor is destroyed; the body around it is unaffected. The sentence representing the goal is matched! Stop!

We will plod along through Duncker's problems pairing elements

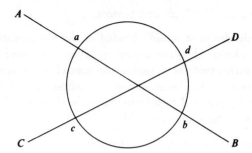

from the domain of the problem through one of the 42 relation words that we took from Basic English. Often coming upon a solution possibility in this way is easy and swift. When one is involved in any problem the number of possible pairs of domain-words is large—it is precisely

(1) $x!$

where x = the number of elements accessible in the domain of the problem. For a single run through the 42 relations in this case one must scan $42x!$ which in the case of a domain with as little as six elements is

(2) $42(6)(5)(4)(3)(2)(1) = 30{,}200$ sentences.

However, in the case in which an accessible element from the domain of the problem is duplicated so it can be related to *itself*, the total number of sentences that need be scanned is

(3) $42(1) = 42$ sentences.

Let us consider the separating of a tangled problem by a clean slice separating the domain to be considered into two identical halves. In the x-ray problem we can leave the esophagus, the throat, the tissues, the stomach wall, the x-ray, and the tumor out in the miasmal fog holding the bag with 30,200 possibilities therein. Instead we choose to take two—two of something: in this case, *fairly* obviously, it must be two rays.

The 42-algorithm is a labored thing except for speedy computers or when the slice is made. After all, in the case of a six-element domain, relating each of the six with another of itself will give as few as

(4) $42(x) = 42(6) = 252$ sentences,

although only the most muddle-headed or the most creative of us will have much choice choosing among relating two esophaguses versus two throats versus two tissues versus two stomach walls versus two x-rays versus two tumors. In the x-ray problem, where one of the relata, the x-ray, is always assumed to be one necessary element, if there are five other elements, the number is still

(5) $42(x) = 42(6) = 252$ sentences.

In terms of the take-two rhythm of this Gordian knot simplification: When each ancient had gone out from preparation into incubation, *re* some invention or discovery, could he have picked his solution out of a list of sentences that numbered 42 in all, when the single element of the problem domain to relate to itself had some special mark of relevance to pick it out? When Mendeleev set out *to arrange the elements* in a good sequence, it was "element dash element" that he needed. When Adams and Leverrier sought *to understand the peculiar orbit* of Uranus, it was "orbit dash orbit" that they needed. Should you seek to solve the problem of weakening the sonic boom, perhaps it is *"noise dash noise"* that you would need to solve that real problem—plus some verificational expertise: taking "a noise under a noise" (the new one under the source of the jet's boom) might deflect the boom or destroy the plane. Who will find out?

8

The relational-algorithm

The worth of the mind consists not in going high,
but in marching orderly.
MONTAIGNE

We are now to the meat of the relational-algorithm, the test of it against a set of problems of some difficulty. These are the problems that Duncker discussed, that he used to make one point or another about, and that he sometimes gave to German college students. We borrow his problems and turn them to our present purpose: to learn to recognize solutions to problems when generated by the relational-algorithm.

THE X-RAY PROBLEM

The first of the problems-to-find is the x-ray problem that we have already talked about (Duncker, 1945, p. 1):

Given a human being with an inoperable stomach tumor, and rays which destroy organic tissue at sufficient intensity, by what procedure can one free him of the tumor by these rays and at the same time avoid destroying the healthy tissue which surrounds it?

The Take-Two-Rays List of Possibilities

Take a ray about a ray.
Take a ray across a ray.
Take a ray after a ray.
Take a ray against a ray.
Take a ray among a ray.
Take a ray and a ray.
Take a ray as a ray.
Take a ray at a ray.
Take a ray because a ray.
Take a ray before a ray.
Take a ray between a ray.
Take a ray but a ray.
Take a ray by a ray.

108

Take a ray down a ray.
Take a ray for a ray.
Take a ray from a ray.
Take a ray if a ray.
Take a ray in a ray.
Take a ray near a ray.
Take a ray not a ray.
Take a ray now a ray.
Take a ray of a ray.
Take a ray off a ray.
Take a ray on a ray.
Take a ray opposite a ray.
Take a ray or a ray.
Take a ray out a ray.
Take a ray over a ray.
Take a ray round a ray.
Take a ray still a ray.
Take a ray so a ray.
Take a ray then a ray.
Take a ray though a ray.
Take a ray through a ray.
Take a ray till a ray.
Take a ray to a ray.
Take a ray under a ray.
Take a ray up a ray.
Take a ray when a ray.
Take a ray where a ray.
Take a ray while a ray.
Take a ray with a ray.

The Body-Ray List of Possibilities

Take the body about the ray.
Take the body across the ray.
Take the body after the ray.
Take the body against the ray.
Take the body among the ray.
Take the body and the ray.
Take the body as the ray.

Take the body at the ray.
Take the body because the ray.
Take the body before the ray.
Take the body between the ray.
Take the body but the ray.
Take the body by the ray.
Take the body down the ray.
Take the body for the ray.
Take the body from the ray.
Take the body if the ray.
Take the body in the ray.
Take the body near the ray.
Take the body not the ray.
Take the body now the ray.
Take the body of the ray.
Take the body off the ray.
Take the body on the ray.
Take the body opposite the ray.
Take the body or the ray.
Take the body out the ray.
Take the body over the ray.
Take the body round the ray.
Take the body still the ray.
Take the body so the ray.
Take the body then the ray.
Take the body though the ray.
Take the body through the ray.
Take the body till the ray.
Take the body to the ray.
Take the body under the ray.
Take the body up the ray.
Take the body when the ray.
Take the body where the ray.
Take the body while the ray.
Take the body with the ray.

As it happens, there are solutions to be found in both sets. For
instance, in the take-two-rays set, there is the possibility of taking one

ray *across* another ray, which is mentioned by Duncker as a good solution when the tumor is at the intersect. In the body-ray list, there is "take the body *round* the ray," which is also a nice solution when the body is rotated with the tumor at the center of rotation, so the cumulative effects of the ray are concentrated at the tumor.

THE CLOCK PROBLEM

In order for a clock to go accurately, the swings of the pendulum must be strictly regular. The duration of the pendulum's swing depends, among other things, on its length, and this, of course, in turn on the temperature. Warming produces expansion and cooling produces contraction, although to different degrees in different materials. Thus every temperature change would change the length of the pendulum. But the clock should go with absolute regularity. How can this be brought about? By the way, the length of the pendulum is defined solely by the shortest distance between the point of suspension and the center of gravity. We are concerned only with this length; for the rest the pendulum may have any appearance at all (Duncker, 1945, p. 6).

The Pendulum-Pendulum List of Possibilities

Take one pendulum about another pendulum.
Take one pendulum across another pendulum.
Take one pendulum after another pendulum.
Take one pendulum against another pendulum.
Take one pendulum among another pendulum.
Take one pendulum and another pendulum.
Take one pendulum as another pendulum.
Take one pendulum at another pendulum.
Take one pendulum because another pendulum.
Take one pendulum before another pendulum.
Take one pendulum between another pendulum.
Take one pendulum but another pendulum.
Take one pendulum by another pendulum.
Take one pendulum down another pendulum.
Take one pendulum for another pendulum.
Take one pendulum from another pendulum.
Take one pendulum if another pendulum.

Take one pendulum in another pendulum.
Take one pendulum near another pendulum.
Take one pendulum not another pendulum.
Take one pendulum now another pendulum.
Take one pendulum of another pendulum.
Take one pendulum off another pendulum.
Take one pendulum on another pendulum.
Take one pendulum opposite another pendulum.
Take one pendulum or another pendulum.
Take one pendulum out another pendulum.
Take one pendulum over another pendulum.
Take one pendulum round another pendulum.
Take one pendulum still another pendulum.
Take one pendulum so another pendulum.
Take one pendulum then another pendulum.
Take one pendulum though another pendulum.
Take one pendulum through another pendulum.
Take one pendulum till another pendulum.
Take one pendulum to another pendulum.
Take one pendulum under another pendulum.
Take one pendulum up another pendulum.
Take one pendulum when another pendulum.
Take one pendulum where another pendulum.
Take one pendulum while another pendulum.
Take one pendulum with another pendulum.

The Material-Pendulum List of Possibilities

Take material about a pendulum.
Take material across a pendulum.
Take material after a pendulum.
Take material against a pendulum.
Take material among a pendulum.
Take material and a pendulum.
Take material as a pendulum.
Take material at a pendulum.
Take material because a pendulum.
Take material before a pendulum.

Take material between a pendulum.
Take material but a pendulum.
Take material by a pendulum.
Take material down a pendulum.
Take material for a pendulum.
Take material from a pendulum.
Take material if a pendulum.
Take material in a pendulum.
Take material near a pendulum.
Take material not a pendulum.
Take material now a pendulum.
Take material of a pendulum.
Take material off a pendulum.
Take material on a pendulum.
Take material opposite a pendulum.
Take material or a pendulum.
Take material out a pendulum.
Take material over a pendulum.
Take material round a pendulum.
Take material still a pendulum.
Take material so a pendulum.
Take material then a pendulum.
Take material though a pendulum.
Take material through a pendulum.
Take material till a pendulum.
Take material to a pendulum.
Take material under a pendulum.
Take material up a pendulum.
Take material when a pendulum.
Take material where a pendulum.
Take material while a pendulum.
Take material with a pendulum.

Duncker recognizes solutions which make the pendulum of materials of two different coefficients of expansion that are arranged in a geometric form so that just as one material expands upwards, the other expands downwards, as in the accompanying figure, used here with permission of the American Psychological Association.

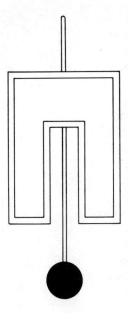

THE RIVER PROBLEM

The problem now is to find "an absolutely unfailing signal to send down a river, i.e., one which cannot catch or be interrupted on the way" (Duncker, 1945, p. 21).

The Water-Water List of Possibilities

Take water about water.
Take water across water.
Take water after water.
Take water against water.
Take water among water.
Take water and water.
Take water as water.
Take water at water.
Take water because water.
Take water before water.
Take water between water.
Take water but water.

Take water by water.
Take water down water.
Take water for water.
Take water from water.
Take water if water.
Take water in water.
Take water near water.
Take water not water.
Take water now water.
Take water of water.
Take water off water.
Take water on water.
Take water opposite water.
Take water or water.
Take water out water.
Take water over water.
Take water round water.
Take water still water.
Take water so water.
Take water then water.
Take water though water.
Take water through water.
Take water till water.
Take water to water.
Take water under water.
Take water up water.
Take water when water.
Take water where water.
Take water while water.
Take water with water.

The River-Water Set of Possibilities

Take river about water.
Take river across water.
Take river after water.
Take river against water.
Take river among water.

Take river and water.
Take river as water.
Take river at water.
Take river because water.
Take river before water.
Take river between water.
Take river but water.
Take river by water.
Take river down water.
Take river for water.
Take river from water.
Take river if water.
Take river in water.
Take river near water.
Take river not water.
Take river now water.
Take river of water.
Take river off water.
Take river on water.
Take river opposite water.
Take river or water.
Take river out water.
Take river over water.
Take river round water.
Take river still water.
Take river so water.
Take river then water.
Take river though water.
Take river through water.
Take river till water.
Take river to water.
Take river under water.
Take river up water.
Take river when water.
Take river where water.
Take river while water.
Take river with water.

You will notice that in the second list I am rather free to put any feasible noun first and another feasible noun second. Just as in the first list, when those nouns are identical, the mind's eye treats this task with a certain symmetry. There is some hint of an interchangeability of parts. Whether one takes river-dash-water or one takes water-dash-river, the set of relations contains a degree of opposites so that "meanings" are preserved though relata are transposed. This hints at a very interesting possibility for the analysis of symmetry in thinking, but this analysis has never been made, to my knowledge.

Well, Duncker liked the very pretty solution to this problem of finding a way to color the water. College students who consider this problem with the relational-algorithm are apt to prefer another, and rather harder solution: they come upon "take water from water" and make the signal be the interruption of the flow of the river they control by building a dam.

THE HANGING-ROPES PROBLEM

Duncker (1945, p. 22) describes this problem as follows.

In a large room, two ropes hang from the ceiling at a considerable distance from one another. One has a small ring on its free end, the other a small hook. A subject has the task of fastening the two ropes together, but this is not possible directly. For the problem is just this: to begin with, how is he to get both ropes in his hands at once? The ropes hang inconveniently far apart.

The Rope-Rope Set of Possibilities

Take a rope about a rope.
Take a rope across a rope.
Take a rope after a rope.
Take a rope against a rope.
Take a rope among a rope.
Take a rope and a rope.
Take a rope as a rope.
Take a rope at a rope.
Take a rope because a rope.
Take a rope before a rope.

Take a rope between a rope.
Take a rope but a rope.
Take a rope by a rope.
Take a rope down a rope.
Take a rope for a rope.
Take a rope from a rope.
Take a rope if a rope.
Take a rope in a rope.
Take a rope near a rope.
Take a rope not a rope.
Take a rope now a rope.
Take a rope of a rope.
Take a rope off a rope.
Take a rope on a rope.
Take a rope opposite a rope.
Take a rope or a rope.
Take a rope out a rope.
Take a rope over a rope.
Take a rope round a rope.
Take a rope still a rope.
Take a rope so a rope.
Take a rope then a rope.
Take a rope though a rope.
Take a rope through a rope.
Take a rope till a rope.
Take a rope to a rope.
Take a rope under a rope.
Take a rope up a rope.
Take a rope when a rope.
Take a rope where a rope.
Take a rope while a rope.
Take a rope with a rope.

The Rope-Hand Set of Possibilities

Take a rope about a hand.
Take a rope across a hand.
Take a rope after a hand.
Take a rope against a hand.

Take a rope among a hand.
Take a rope and a hand.
Take a rope as a hand.
Take a rope at a hand.
Take a rope because a hand.
Take a rope before a hand.
Take a rope between a hand.
Take a rope but a hand.
Take a rope by a hand.
Take a rope down a hand.
Take a rope for a hand.
Take a rope from a hand.
Take a rope if a hand.
Take a rope in a hand.
Take a rope near a hand.
Take a rope not a hand.
Take a rope now a hand.
Take a rope of a hand.
Take a rope off a hand.
Take a rope on a hand.
Take a rope opposite a hand.
Take a rope or a hand.
Take a rope out a hand.
Take a rope over a hand.
Take a rope round a hand.
Take a rope still a hand.
Take a rope so a hand.
Take a rope then a hand.
Take a rope though a hand.
Take a rope through a hand.
Take a rope till a hand.
Take a rope to a hand.
Take a rope under a hand.
Take a rope up a hand.
Take a rope when a hand.
Take a rope where a hand.
Take a rope while a hand.
Take a rope with a hand.

The solution that Duncker mentioned to this problem is to swing one rope so it can be caught while holding the other one.

THE FOUR-TRIANGLES PROBLEM

On page 26 of his monograph, Duncker mentioned this problem: four equilateral triangles are to be constructed out of six matches.

The Triangle-Triangle Set of Possibilities

Take a triangle about a triangle.
Take a triangle across a triangle.
Take a triangle after a triangle.
Take a triangle against a triangle.
Take a triangle among a triangle.
Take a triangle and a triangle.
Take a triangle as a triangle.
Take a triangle at a triangle.
Take a triangle because a triangle.
Take a triangle before a triangle.
Take a triangle between a triangle.
Take a triangle but a triangle.
Take a triangle by a triangle.
Take a triangle down a triangle.
Take a triangle for a triangle.
Take a triangle from a triangle.
Take a triangle if a triangle.
Take a triangle in a triangle.
Take a triangle near a triangle.
Take a triangle not a triangle.
Take a triangle now a triangle.
Take a triangle of a triangle.
Take a triangle off a triangle.
Take a triangle on a triangle.
Take a triangle opposite a triangle.
Take a triangle or a triangle.
Take a triangle out a triangle.
Take a triangle over a triangle.
Take a triangle round a triangle.

Take a triangle still a triangle.
Take a triangle so a triangle.
Take a triangle then a triangle.
Take a triangle though a triangle.
Take a triangle through a triangle.
Take a triangle till a triangle.
Take a triangle to a triangle.
Take a triangle under a triangle.
Take a triangle up a triangle.
Take a triangle when a triangle.
Take a triangle where a triangle.
Take a triangle while a triangle.
Take a triangle with a triangle.

The Match-Triangle Set of Possibilities

Take matches about a triangle.
Take matches across a triangle.
Take matches after a triangle.
Take matches against a triangle.
Take matches among a triangle.
Take matches and a triangle.
Take matches as a triangle.
Take matches at a triangle.
Take matches because a triangle.
Take matches before a triangle.
Take matches between a triangle.
Take matches but a triangle.
Take matches by a triangle.
Take matches down a triangle.
Take matches for a triangle.
Take matches from a triangle.
Take matches if a triangle.
Take matches in a triangle.
Take matches near a triangle.
Take matches not a triangle.
Take matches now a triangle.
Take matches of a triangle.

Take matches off a triangle.
Take matches on a triangle.
Take matches opposite a triangle.
Take matches or a triangle.
Take matches out a triangle.
Take matches over a triangle.
Take matches round a triangle.
Take matches still a triangle.
Take matches so a triangle.
Take matches then a triangle.
Take matches though a triangle.
Take matches through a triangle.
Take matches till a triangle.
Take matches to a triangle.
Take matches under a triangle.
Take matches up a triangle.
Take matches when a triangle.
Take matches where a triangle.
Take matches while a triangle.
Take matches with a triangle.

The solution to this problem that is mentioned by Duncker is to construct a tetrahedron. It is a three-dimensional figure, with three matches forming a triangle flat on the table, and the other three matches up into the air so they all meet at a point while each has its other end at a corner of the triangle. College students using the relational-algorithm have found two other solutions. One comes out of the operation of taking two matches—break each match into two, then easily construct four triangles of the twelve pieces. Students who come upon "take a triangle on another triangle" may offer the solution depicted in the figure on the next page.

THE DOOR PROBLEM

On page 26 of his monograph, Duncker described this problem: "A door is to be constructed so as to open toward both sides. How can this be attained?" He showed a figure of a door attached to a hinge, with the hinge in turn attached to the wall.

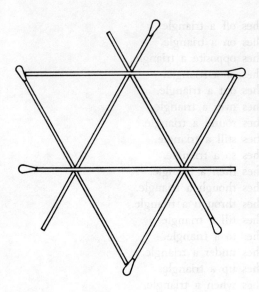

The Hinge-Hinge Set of Possibilities

Take a hinge about a hinge.
Take a hinge across a hinge.
Take a hinge after a hinge.
Take a hinge against a hinge.
Take a hinge among a hinge.
Take a hinge and a hinge.
Take a hinge as a hinge.
Take a hinge at a hinge.
Take a hinge because a hinge.
Take a hinge before a hinge.
Take a hinge between a hinge.
Take a hinge but a hinge.
Take a hinge by a hinge.
Take a hinge down a hinge.
Take a hinge for a hinge.
Take a hinge from a hinge.
Take a hinge if a hinge.
Take a hinge in a hinge.
Take a hinge near a hinge.

Take a hinge not a hinge.
Take a hinge now a hinge.
Take a hinge of a hinge.
Take a hinge off a hinge.
Take a hinge on a hinge.
Take a hinge opposite a hinge.
Take a hinge or a hinge.
Take a hinge out a hinge.
Take a hinge over a hinge.
Take a hinge round a hinge.
Take a hinge still a hinge.
Take a hinge so a hinge.
Take a hinge then a hinge.
Take a hinge though a hinge.
Take a hinge through a hinge.
Take a hinge till a hinge.
Take a hinge to a hinge.
Take a hinge under a hinge.
Take a hinge up a hinge.
Take a hinge when a hinge.
Take a hinge where a hinge.
Take a hinge while a hinge.
Take a hinge with a hinge.

It is time now to become more audacious, taking no hinge at all, but the door and the wall.

The Door-Wall Set of Possibilities

Take a door about a wall.
Take a door across a wall.
Take a door after a wall.
Take a door against a wall.
Take a door among a wall.
Take a door and a wall.
Take a door as a wall.
Take a door at a wall.
Take a door because a wall.
Take a door before a wall.

Take a door between a wall.
Take a door but a wall.
Take a door by a wall.
Take a door down a wall.
Take a door for a wall.
Take a door from a wall.
Take a door if a wall.
Take a door in a wall.
Take a door near a wall.
Take a door not a wall.
Take a door now a wall.
Take a door of a wall.
Take a door off a wall.
Take a door on a wall.
Take a door opposite a wall.
Take a door or a wall.
Take a door out a wall.
Take a door over a wall.
Take a door round a wall.
Take a door still a wall.
Take a door so a wall.
Take a door then a wall.
Take a door though a wall.
Take a door through a wall.
Take a door till a wall.
Take a door to a wall.
Take a door under a wall.
Take a door up a wall.
Take a door when a wall.
Take a door where a wall.
Take a door while a wall.
Take a door with a wall.

The solution that Duncker enjoys applying to this problem is, indeed, to use two hinges on each other so that one serves the rotation of the other. No solution is evident to anyone I have tested in the door-wall list, for a hinge is missing and it seems to be needed. Inspecting a hingeless list for this problem is both too bold and also rather stupid.

We may be pleased that no solution comes out of that list and may be reminded of the wisdom of noticing that even the trees do not grow to the sky.

THE MOUNTAIN-CLIMBER PROBLEM

On page 56 Duncker describes the famous problem of the mountain climber:

On a mountain trip, on which descent was by the same path as had been the ascent of the previous day, I ask myself whether there must be a spot en route at which I must find myself at exactly the same time on the descent as on the ascent. It was of course assumed that ascent and descent took place at about the same time of day, say from five to twelve o'clock—but without further probing I could arrive at no conclusive insight.

The Climber-Climber Set of Possibilities

Take a climber about a climber.
Take a climber across a climber.
Take a climber after a climber.
Take a climber against a climber.
Take a climber among a climber.
Take a climber and a climber.
Take a climber as a climber.
Take a climber at a climber.
Take a climber because a climber.
Take a climber before a climber
Take a climber between a climber.
Take a climber but a climber.
Take a climber by a climber.
Take a climber down a climber.
Take a climber for a climber.
Take a climber from a climber.
Take a climber if a climber.
Take a climber in a climber.
Take a climber near a climber.
Take a climber not a climber.
Take a climber now a climber.
Take a climber of a climber.

Take a climber off a climber.
Take a climber on a climber.
Take a climber opposite a climber.
Take a climber or a climber.
Take a climber out a climber.
Take a climber over a climber.
Take a climber round a climber.
Take a climber still a climber.
Take a climber so a climber.
Take a climber then a climber.
Take a climber though a climber.
Take a climber through a climber.
Take a climber till a climber.
Take a climber to a climber.
Take a climber under a climber.
Take a climber up a climber.
Take a climber when a climber.
Take a climber where a climber.
Take a climber while a climber.
Take a climber with a climber.

The Ascent-Descent Set of Possibilities

Take ascent about descent.
Take ascent across descent.
Take ascent after descent.
Take ascent against descent.
Take ascent among descent.
Take ascent and descent.
Take ascent as descent.
Take ascent at descent.
Take ascent because descent.
Take ascent before descent.
Take ascent between descent.
Take ascent but descent.
Take ascent by descent.
Take ascent down descent.
Take ascent for descent.
Take ascent from descent.

Take ascent if descent.
Take ascent in descent.
Take ascent near descent.
Take ascent not descent.
Take ascent now descent.
Take ascent of descent.
Take ascent off descent.
Take ascent on descent.
Take ascent opposite descent.
Take ascent or descent.
Take ascent out descent.
Take ascent over descent.
Take ascent round descent.
Take ascent still descent.
Take ascent so descent.
Take ascent then descent.
Take ascent though descent.
Take ascent through descent.
Take ascent till descent.
Take ascent to descent.
Take ascent under descent.
Take ascent up descent.
Take ascent when descent.
Take ascent where descent.
Take ascent while descent.
Take ascent with descent.

In the monograph, Duncker fancied the solution to this problem as being the image of one climber going up as the other climber went down. Thus they must pass at some specific place at some specific time. Arthur Koestler (1964, p. 184) also solved this problem when in the mind's eye two travellers passed on that mountain path going in opposite directions. Alas though, one might come up with that image—or indeed have Disney's people animate a cartoon that displayed such a crossing —but still not come to the recognition that the work was done. Wallas (1926) put it that "Verification with her lame foot and painful step must follow Illumination." This is true for spontaneous insights, and no less true for algorithmic *in*sights, and *near*sights, and *not*sights, and *now*sights, and *of*sights, and *off*sights . . . and, of course, even algorithmic *over*sights.

THE PROBLEM OF THE CIRCLE-IN-THE-SQUARE

On page 59 of the monograph, Duncker gives a problem that has the appearance of a mathematical problem-to-find: "Measure the side of a square in terms of the radius of an inscribed circle." His subjects were also given the (misleading) figure reproduced here, with permission of the American Psychological Association.

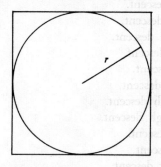

Undaunted, we can run through these lists.

The Radius-Radius List

Take a radius about a radius.
Take a radius across a radius.
Take a radius after a radius.
Take a radius against a radius.
Take a radius among a radius.
Take a radius and a radius.
Take a radius as a radius.
Take a radius at a radius.
Take a radius because a radius.
Take a radius before a radius.
Take a radius between a radius.
Take a radius but a radius.
Take a radius by a radius.
Take a radius down a radius.

Take a radius for a radius.
Take a radius from a radius.
Take a radius if a radius.
Take a radius in a radius.
Take a radius near a radius.
Take a radius not a radius.
Take a radius now a radius.
Take a radius of a radius.
Take a radius off a radius.
Take a radius on a radius.
Take a radius opposite a radius.
Take a radius or a radius.
Take a radius out a radius.
Take a radius over a radius.
Take a radius round a radius.
Take a radius still a radius.
Take a radius so a radius.
Take a radius then a radius.
Take a radius though a radius.
Take a radius through a radius.
Take a radius till a radius.
Take a radius to a radius.
Take a radius under a radius.
Take a radius up a radius.
Take a radius when a radius.
Take a radius where a radius.
Take a radius while a radius.
Take a radius with a radius.

The Radius-Square List of Possibilities

Take radius about square.
Take radius across square.
Take radius after square.
Take radius against square.
Take radius among square.
Take radius and square.
Take radius as square.
Take radius at square.

Take radius because square.
Take radius before square.
Take radius between square.
Take radius but square.
Take radius by square.
Take radius down square.
Take radius for square.
Take radius from square.
Take radius if square.
Take radius in square.
Take radius near square.
Take radius not square.
Take radius now square.
Take radius of square.
Take radius off square.
Take radius on square.
Take radius opposite square.
Take radius or square.
Take radius out square.
Take radius over square.
Take radius round square.
Take radius still square.
Take radius so square.
Take radius then square.
Take radius though square.
Take radius through square.
Take radius till square.
Take radius to square.
Take radius under square.
Take radius up square.
Take radius when square.
Take radius where square.
Take radius while square.
Take radius with square.

The solution favored by Duncker is to rotate a radius into a position parallel to a side in order to be able to "read off" that the side of the square is equal to two radii of the inscribed circle. One might come to that from "take a radius down a radius" or "take radius against square."

THE GIMLET PROBLEM

On page 86 of Duncker's monograph is this problem: "Three cords are to be hung side by side from a wooden ledge. On the table lie, among other things, two short screw hooks and a gimlet."

The Cord-Cord Set of Possibilities

Take a cord about cords.
Take a cord across cords.
Take a cord after cords.
Take a cord against cords.
Take a cord among cords.
Take a cord and cords.
Take a cord as cords.
Take a cord at cords.
Take a cord because cords.
Take a cord before cords.
Take a cord between cords.
Take a cord but cords.
Take a cord by cords.
Take a cord down cords.
Take a cord for cords.
Take a cord from cords.
Take a cord if cords.
Take a cord in cords.
Take a cord near cords.
Take a cord not cords.
Take a cord now cords.
Take a cord of cords.
Take a cord off cords.
Take a cord on cords.
Take a cord opposite cords.
Take a cord or cords.

Take a cord out cords.
Take a cord over cords.
Take a cord round cords.
Take a cord still cords.
Take a cord so cords.
Take a cord then cords.
Take a cord though cords.
Take a cord through cords.
Take a cord till cords.
Take a cord to cords.
Take a cord under cords.
Take a cord up cords.
Take a cord when cords.
Take a cord where cords.
Take a cord while cords.
Take a cord with cords.

The Gimlet-Hooks Set of Possibilities

Take gimlet about hooks.
Take gimlet across hooks.
Take gimlet after hooks.
Take gimlet against hooks.
Take gimlet among hooks.
Take gimlet and hooks.
Take gimlet as hooks.
Take gimlet at hooks.
Take gimlet because hooks.
Take gimlet before hooks.
Take gimlet between hooks.
Take gimlet but hooks.
Take gimlet by hooks.
Take gimlet down hooks.
Take gimlet for hooks.
Take gimlet from hooks.
Take gimlet if hooks.
Take gimlet in hooks.
Take gimlet near hooks.

Take gimlet not hooks.
Take gimlet now hooks.
Take gimlet of hooks.
Take gimlet off hooks.
Take gimlet on hooks.
Take gimlet opposite hooks.
Take gimlet or hooks.
Take gimlet out hooks.
Take gimlet over hooks.
Take gimlet round hooks.
Take gimlet still hooks.
Take gimlet so hooks.
Take gimlet then hooks.
Take gimlet though hooks.
Take gimlet through hooks.
Take gimlet till hooks.
Take gimlet to hooks.
Take gimlet under hooks.
Take gimlet up hooks.
Take gimlet when hooks.
Take gimlet where hooks.
Take gimlet while hooks.
Take gimlet with hooks.

Duncker gives as the solution to this problem: hang a cord from each screw hook and a third from the gimlet. Students get to other "solutions" through these lists of actions. "Take a cord under cords" suggests hanging two cords from one cord, and "Take gimlet and hooks" suggests Duncker's solution. Hanging the three cords together from a single hook, say, does seem unfair—it seems too simple a solution, that something more complicated is necessary (the old inventor's inhibition!).

THE BOX PROBLEM

On the door, at the height of the eyes, three small candles are to be put side by side. On the cluttered table is a few tacks and three little pasteboard boxes (Duncker, 1945, p. 86).

The Candle-Candles Set of Possibilities

Take a candle about candles.
Take a candle across candles.
Take a candle after candles.
Take a candle against candles.
Take a candle among candles.
Take a candle and candles.
Take a candle as candles.
Take a candle at candles.
Take a candle because candles.
Take a candle before candles.
Take a candle between candles.
Take a candle but candles.
Take a candle by candles.
Take a candle down candles.
Take a candle for candles.
Take a candle from candles.
Take a candle if candles.
Take a candle in candles.
Take a candle near candles.
Take a candle not candles.
Take a candle now candles.
Take a candle of candles.
Take a candle off candles.
Take a candle on candles.
Take a candle opposite candles.
Take a candle or candles.
Take a candle out candles.
Take a candle over candles.
Take a candle round candles.
Take a candle still candles.
Take a candle so candles.
Take a candle then candles.
Take a candle though candles.
Take a candle through candles.
Take a candle till candles.
Take a candle to candles.

Take a candle under candles.
Take a candle up candles.
Take a candle when candles.
Take a candle where candles.
Take a candle while candles.
Take a candle with candles.

The Tack-Box Set of Possibilities

Take tack about box.
Take tack across box.
Take tack after box.
Take tack against box.
Take tack among box.
Take tack and box.
Take tack as box.
Take tack at box.
Take tack because box.
Take tack before box.
Take tack between box.
Take tack but box.
Take tack by box.
Take tack down box.
Take tack for box.
Take tack from box.
Take tack if box.
Take tack in box.
Take tack near box.
Take tack not box.
Take tack now box.
Take tack of box.
Take tack off box.
Take tack on box.
Take tack opposite box.
Take tack or box.
Take tack out box.
Take tack over box.
Take tack round box.
Take tack still box.

Take tack so box.
Take tack then box.
Take tack though box.
Take tack through box.
Take tack till box.
Take tack to box.
Take tack under box.
Take tack up box.
Take tack when box.
Take tack where box.
Take tack while box.
Take tack with box.

Duncker's solution, in our elementary idiom, is to take a tack through a box, against a wall, with a candle on the box. One ends with three boxes stuck to the wall, each with a candle erect upon a box. Rather a pretty picture. But to make a box a platform for an erect candle, one has first to "take a match against the wall" (to get it burning) and then "take a candle over a match" (to melt the candle a bit) so that one can finally "take a candle on a box." The pedestrian piling up of small steps that fall from the algorithm that finally comes to make up a presumably fluent complex act indicates not only how simple the acts are that underlie the solutions to these, and perhaps many other, problems—it also has a kind of macabre humor. Some students prefer a much more elegant solution to this problem, needing no box and no tack. We come to "take a candle against candles" and may import the melting of the candlewax at this point, doing enough melting so that the three candles become stuck to each other and then stuck right to the wall. How like Duncker's *par force* solutions are the solutions that suggest themselves as one goes through the lists, particularly the "take-two" lists in which two of the same objects are interrelated!

THE PLIERS PROBLEM

A board (perhaps 8 inches broad) is to be made firm on two supports (as "flower stand or the like"). On the table lie, among other things, two iron joints (for fastening bars and the like on stands), a wooden bar perhaps 8 inches long (as the one "support") and the critical object, the pliers (Duncker, 1945, p. 86).

The Joint-Joint List of Possibilities

Take joint about joint.
Take joint across joint.
Take joint after joint.
Take joint against joint.
Take joint among joint.
Take joint and joint.
Take joint as joint.
Take joint at joint.
Take joint because joint.
Take joint before joint.
Take joint between joint.
Take joint but joint.
Take joint by joint.
Take joint down joint.
Take joint for joint.
Take joint from joint.
Take joint if joint.
Take joint in joint.
Take joint near joint.
Take joint not joint.
Take joint now joint.
Take joint of joint.
Take joint off joint.
Take joint on joint.
Take joint opposite joint.
Take joint or joint.
Take joint out joint.
Take joint over joint.
Take joint round joint.
Take joint still joint.
Take joint so joint.
Take joint then joint.
Take joint though joint.
Take joint through joint.
Take joint till joint.
Take joint to joint.

Take joint under joint.
Take joint up joint.
Take joint when joint.
Take joint where joint.
Take joint while joint.
Take joint with joint.

The Pliers-Bar List of Possibilities

Take pliers about bar.
Take pliers across bar.
Take pliers after bar.
Take pliers against bar.
Take pliers among bar.
Take pliers and bar.
Take pliers as bar.
Take pliers at bar.
Take pliers because bar.
Take pliers before bar.
Take pliers between bar.
Take pliers but bar.
Take pliers by bar.
Take pliers down bar.
Take pliers for bar.
Take pliers from bar.
Take pliers if bar.
Take pliers in bar.
Take pliers near bar.
Take pliers not bar.
Take pliers now bar.
Take pliers of bar.
Take pliers off bar.
Take pliers on bar.
Take pliers opposite bar.
Take pliers or bar.
Take pliers out bar.
Take pliers over bar.
Take pliers round bar.
Take pliers still bar.

Take pliers so bar.
Take pliers then bar.
Take pliers though bar.
Take pliers through bar.
Take pliers till bar.
Take pliers to bar.
Take pliers under bar.
Take pliers up bar.
Take pliers when bar.
Take pliers where bar.
Take pliers while bar.
Take pliers with bar.

Duncker fancied using the bar as one support for the board, the pliers as the other support ("take the board on the bar and take the board on the pliers," in our halting but apparently inexorable idiom). The joint-joint list was made because we had two joints, but only one of anything else, and there was no obvious way to break into two parts some available single thing, nor any desire to test the relating of one part of the board to another part of the board, say. Should the joints be the appropriate size, taking a joint over a joint might allow the double-joint to be used, instead of the pliers, as the second support.

THE WEIGHT PROBLEM

A pendulum, consisting of a cord and a weight, is to be hung from a nail (for experiments on motion). To this end the nail must be driven into the wall. On the table, among other things, lies the crucial object: a weight.

So, Duncker (p. 86) would have us take the weight in some relation to the nail and the wall.

The Weight-Nail List of Possibilities

Take weight about nail.
Take weight across nail.
Take weight after nail.
Take weight against nail.
Take weight among nail.
Take weight and nail.
Take weight as nail.

Take weight at nail.
Take weight because nail.
Take weight before nail.
Take weight between nail.
Take weight but nail.
Take weight by nail.
Take weight down nail.
Take weight for nail.
Take weight from nail.
Take weight if nail.
Take weight in nail.
Take weight near nail.
Take weight not nail.
Take weight now nail.
Take weight of nail.
Take weight off nail.
Take weight on nail.
Take weight opposite nail.
Take weight or nail.
Take weight out nail.
Take weight over nail.
Take weight round nail.
Take weight still nail.
Take weight so nail.
Take weight then nail.
Take weight though nail.
Take weight through nail.
Take weight till nail.
Take weight to nail.
Take weight under nail.
Take weight up nail.
Take weight when nail.
Take weight where nail.
Take weight while nail.
Take weight with nail.

The solution Duncker wants is to hammer the nail into the wall by using the weight. ("Take weight against nail," while one takes nail against wall.) This particular problem get from students the immediate wish to have a hammer to get the blasphemous nail into the wall. But all they have is a pendulum. After knowing this sort of listing, they may come to "take pendulum as hammer," which is but a step from the Duncker solution, but not uniformly as easy a step.

The Pendulum-Hammer List of Possibilities

Take pendulum about hammer.
Take pendulum across hammer.
Take pendulum after hammer.
Take pendulum against hammer.
Take pendulum among hammer.
Take pendulum and hammer.
Take pendulum as hammer.
Take pendulum at hammer.
Take pendulum because hammer.
Take pendulum before hammer.
Take pendulum between hammer.
Take pendulum but hammer.
Take pendulum by hammer.
Take pendulum down hammer.
Take pendulum for hammer.
Take pendulum from hammer.
Take pendulum if hammer.
Take pendulum in hammer.
Take pendulum near hammer.
Take pendulum not hammer.
Take pendulum now hammer.
Take pendulum of hammer.
Take pendulum off hammer.
Take pendulum on hammer.
Take pendulum opposite hammer.
Take pendulum or hammer.
Take pendulum out hammer.
Take pendulum over hammer.
Take pendulum round hammer.
Take pendulum still hammer.
Take pendulum so hammer.

142

Take pendulum then hammer.
Take pendulum though hammer.
Take pendulum through hammer.
Take pendulum till hammer.
Take pendulum to hammer.
Take pendulum under hammer.
Take pendulum up hammer.
Take pendulum when hammer.
Take pendulum where hammer.
Take pendulum while hammer.
Take pendulum with hammer.

THE PAPERCLIP PROBLEM

On p. 87 of his monograph, Duncker presents the following problem: a piece of white cardboard with four black squares fastened to it is to be hung on an eyelet screwed into the low ceiling ("for visual experiments"). On the table lie paperclips, among other things.

The Cardboard-Eyelet Set of Possibilities

Take cardboard about eyelet.
Take cardboard across eyelet.
Take cardboard after eyelet.
Take cardboard against eyelet.
Take cardboard among eyelet.
Take cardboard and eyelet.
Take cardboard as eyelet.
Take cardboard at eyelet.
Take cardboard because eyelet.
Take cardboard before eyelet.
Take cardboard between eyelet.
Take cardboard but eyelet.
Take cardboard by eyelet.
Take cardboard down eyelet.
Take cardboard for eyelet.
Take cardboard from eyelet.
Take cardboard if eyelet.
Take cardboard in eyelet.

Take cardboard near eyelet.
Take cardboard not eyelet.
Take cardboard now eyelet.
Take cardboard of eyelet.
Take cardboard off eyelet.
Take cardboard on eyelet.
Take cardboard opposite eyelet.
Take cardboard or eyelet.
Take cardboard out eyelet.
Take cardboard over eyelet.
Take cardboard round eyelet.
Take cardboard still eyelet.
Take cardboard so eyelet.
Take cardboard then eyelet.
Take cardboard though eyelet.
Take cardboard through eyelet.
Take cardboard till eyelet.
Take cardboard to eyelet.
Take cardboard under eyelet.
Take cardboard up eyelet.
Take cardboard when eyelet.
Take cardboard where eyelet.
Take cardboard while eyelet.
Take cardboard with eyelet.

Students may verbalize the problem this way: I have a paperclip, but I need a joint between eyelet and cardboard.

The Paperclip-Joint List of Possibilities

Take paperclip about joint.
Take paperclip across joint.
Take paperclip after joint.
Take paperclip against joint.
Take paperclip among joint.
Take paperclip and joint.
Take paperclip as joint.
Take paperclip at joint.
Take paperclip because joint.

Take paperclip before joint.
Take paperclip between joint.
Take paperclip but joint.
Take paperclip by joint.
Take paperclip down joint.
Take paperclip for joint.
Take paperclip from joint.
Take paperclip if joint.
Take paperclip in joint.
Take paperclip near joint.
Take paperclip not joint.
Take paperclip now joint.
Take paperclip of joint.
Take paperclip off joint.
Take paperclip on joint.
Take paperclip opposite joint.
Take paperclip or joint.
Take paperclip out joint.
Take paperclip over joint.
Take paperclip round joint.
Take paperclip still joint.
Take paperclip so joint.
Take paperclip then joint.
Take paperclip though joint.
Take paperclip through joint.
Take paperclip till joint.
Take paperclip to joint.
Take paperclip under joint.
Take paperclip up joint.
Take paperclip when joint.
Take paperclip where joint.
Take paperclip while joint.
Take paperclip with joint.

The solution Duncker sought was this: a paperclip is unbent, one end is fastened to the eyelet, and the other is put through the cardboard.

In the previous five problems (the gimlet problem, the box problem, the pliers problem, the weight problem, and the paperclip problem)

Duncker had decided on the "correct" solution a priori. "Of course, a problem is counted as 'correctly' solved only when it was solved by the use of the crucial object, which as stated, was always the best and simplest of the possible solutions" (p. 87). Thus in the gimlet problem he would accept hanging a cord from each screw hook and one from the gimlet, but would not accept hanging three cords from a single hook. In the box problem he would accept taking a tack through each box, against the wall, each with a candle on it; he would not accept fusing the candles to each other and to the wall. In the pliers problem he would accept as a solution taking the board on the bar and the board on the pliers, but he would not accept making a stand of the joints, or breaking the bar in half to give two supports from that one. In the weight problem, he would accept hammering the nail into the wall by using the weight as a hammer—but not a shoe. In the paper-clip problem he would accept taking the paperclip as a joint between cardboard and eyelet, but would not accept refastening the eyelet to the ceiling through the cardboard, making paperclips superfluous.

Duncker was under the great strain imposed by his hypothesis that functional fixedness is always the barrier to solution. Hence he defined solutions in terms of the surmounting of some barrier he put in the way of solution. That barrier conformed to his understanding of the concept of functional fixedness. He cannot be blamed for a gratuitous decision concerning what solution was the best and the simplest, for he was quite free of any serious concern about specifying the set of all possible solutions to a problem, and when he said "the possible solutions" he merely meant all those that were known to him. Methods of analysis always carry with them the danger of turning meanings to one's own ends, ruling out other possibilities as unspeakable. The more arbitrary and specialized the basic decisions are, the greater must be that hazard.

The last few problems were rigged by Duncker to allow the study of functional fixedness. The plan was to show that an object is not quickly chosen to be used for a new purpose. In these problems, Duncker notes sadly that the subject makes rationalizations for why he did not use the "critical object" that lies outside his focal view—but Duncker denies that one should expect any illumination from the post hoc rationalizations of a subject. Indeed, when the critical object was pointed out, subjects did not feel they had been victims of a false interpretation of the experimental situation—rather it was as if "the scales had fallen from their eyes" when the critical object was pointed out. We may wonder that Duncker had the confidence to deny "rationalizations" of why the critical object was not used, but to accept "statements" of falling scales. Perhaps things were different in those ancient days.

9
Conclusion

*After April, 1879 . . . [Edison] . . . seemed to become
more 'disciplined' and was gradually converted into a
scientific investigator.*
M. JOSEPHSON (1959, p. 207)

We now stand nearly a century after Francis Galton's walk along
Pall Mall with three small gains from it. He caught a glimpse of the
recurrence of the contents of consciousness. We have capitalized on
the forms and contents of that recurrence to fashion three algorithms
for the use of anyone with the patience and desire to use them. Of
course, much needs yet to be found out, but there are things we now
can do. It is long division all over again. We can even consider teaching
this all in elementary school.

To make memory more nearly perfect, use portable memory maps.
For understanding prose, cross out the content words and indwell the
bare form that remains. To write a first draft of an article in an hour,
cross out an article's content words and methodically fill in the blanks
with the content of your work. To create, invent, discover, problem-
solve, or to pop out from incubation into illumination, the thing to use
is the algorithm of the 42 little words. It helps you ripple through a
wide set of potential actions which then must be evaluated in a stage
like "verification" as the ancients knew it.

Here is what we do *not* know: features of recurrence as it occurs
in Nature. Finding out about that seems as hard to me today as it may
have seemed to Galton, who went on to more accessible things.

Why is natural memory so faulty? From our present viewpoint we
can objectify memory maps and carry them about, so that memories
can be unearthed by finding *where* they were put wrapped in a vivid
image. In natural memory we may have neither the "location" of a
memory nor any "vividness" to let it show. As we get old, memory of
very old things becomes vivid, but recent things are lost. Certain kinds
of damage to the brain selectively attack short-term versus long-term
memory. In Nature it all is rather detailed and complex.

Similarly, why is understanding difficult for some of us, and composi-

147

tion too? We now know something of how to disentangle the form from the content of material made of words. In natural reading or writing, we tend to get burdened with content, having the form become a jumble. Much seems to be carried on the sequence of words, and without care sequence becomes disordered.

Lastly, why do some of us have a clever idea once in a while, but not whenever we would like to? The answer is that in the natural state we get stuck on certain forms of action, bringing all our efforts to bear on a fraction of the set of possibilities. Now we have an algorithm for scanning a larger set of possibilities. We assume that all is a recycling of a small set of forms.

Why don't chimpanzees talk? Vygotsky (1962) thought it was because they were too visual, but no one I know has reported long conversations with chimpanzees at the zoo in the dark. Some brain damage leaves much intact; other brain damage has a widely disruptive impact on "mental" functioning. The best physical image of such a strange state of affairs is the status of the field of an insulated magnet. Up to some limit, symmetric damage or insulation will leave the form of the field intact. On the other hand, a tiny deformation of the shape of the magnet will make a striking change in the field. However, the *status ante* can be mostly recovered by adding insulation to unaffected areas so that at the end the symmetry will be restored, as will the integrity of the field. It is perhaps strange that the Gestalt psychologists of the early years of this century did not treat topics such as this one in this manner, but I fear such treatment was too abstract for them— they thought that the competitors were the dying Introspectionists of Germany and the vigorous young Behaviorists of the United States. Neither of those camps then had abstract generality as a long suit, and the Gestalters were out to reshape the existing psychology rather than dwell on more basic matters.

Like physics before Copernicus, psychology still holds dear the contention that (psychological) laws can be derived from "intelligible principles" (Frank, 1961). Now that mathematical thinking is overrunning psychology, there is some hope that less egocentric laws will be found; but the digital computer is so interesting and complex a toy it may divert our attention for another hundred years. Galton, too, was easily led from his path by shinier marbles; he would understand. It is the complexity of digital computers that may be most distracting, but it should be recognized that contemporary work on computer simulation has made an invaluable contribution to renewed speculation on the hardest problems in the study of human thinking (see, for example, the article by Newell, Shaw, and Simon, 1958).

Theories have two functions: generating the facts and making people happy. Many different stories of the reasons for things have made people happy at one time or another, but the hard-headed initial requirement of a theory must be that it generates the facts fairly well. Scientific theories usually make people happy only through their elegance and their fruits; in psychology a different requirement still fogs the air. For most adults, psychological theory must include room for some old ideas: consciousness, personality, motivation, habit, and so on. Even the worst of us might admit, however, that such concepts might have no status in the theoretical psychology written by a sapient honeybee, or a wayward computer.

The trouble with developing a theory that meets the arduous test of generating facts without ambiguity is that nobody knows how to *do* it. Long ago, Celsus made the eternally wise observation that medicines and cures are first found, and then the reasons for their efficacy are understood; not that causes of diseases are first understood, and from such understanding medicines and cures follow.

The reviewer of a modern edition of Kepler's "The Six-Cornered Snowflake" (Barnett, 1967) pointed out with grace that while the problem of "why" a snowflake has six corners remains unsolved to this day, Kepler did proceed by using the strongest methods of modern theorists: symmetry and analogy. Further, "why six" may be a simple question, but progress occurs when answers, not questions, are simple.

In accordance with the view that the deep importance of simple answers might extend as far into fog as where we are, consider now a simple analogy for building a theory. The turnkey model supposes that there are a finite number of answers that are like keys; there is a large number of questions that are like locks. To "build" a theory is to find which locks are opened by which keys. It is very topsy-turvy, of course. The job of the theorist is to find some beautiful, or elegant, or merely simple, keys—and then scout around for beautiful questions that available keys unlock.

However, even a turnkey must keep his wits about him lest he fail to recognize when a key does fit a lock. One of the most inventive of men was Father Scheiner, a contemporary and, for good or ill, a reluctant enemy of Galileo. He measured the curvature of the anterior surface of the cornea of the eye. His method was really the same that Newton later used to invent the reflecting telescope. The fact of the matter is that warped mirrors give distorted images—nicely polished perfect spherical mirrors distort, or change, the size of the image only, proportional to the angle of curvature.

Father Scheiner had some marbles. The set of shiny round balls varied in regard to the diameter of the individual balls. Scheiner sat his people down facing a window with a cross on it—that cross, of course, being visible upon the cornea as a reflected image. Then Father Scheiner took his bag of marbles and placed one or another marble in the space between eye and nose, stopping when the image of the cross reflected from the eye was about equal in size to the image of the cross as reflected from the marble. It is easy to measure a marble; from it can easily be deduced the angle of curvature of the anterior surface of the cornea, *quid est demonstrandum*. When we look very closely at inventions, we have grim cause to recognize that, though the idea "take a marble on the nose" might "solve" the problem of measuring corneas, it is not at all insured that anyone has the wit unfailingly to recognize it as a solution—that is, to match it to a question. If anyone did, what else might he invent or discover in a bag of marbles?

From the point of view of the turnkey model of theory and discovery, the limit to the number of keys (answers) is unknown. Similarly, there is no charted course to arrive at locks (questions). Consider the analogous problem in physics for a moment. Galileo may have played with the law of falling bodies in thought, but in action he played with rolling marbles down inclined grooves. (Heaven help us to avoid hard and unclear things to do!) Given the rules of marbles rolling down grooves, Galileo generalized the rule. To generalize is to assert that *this* thing is just like all *those* things which are too far away to measure directly.

What would be the laws of a universe in which psychology would be very easy? Is that universe very far from our own? Well, it may be rather far from the universe with psychology bounded by William James at one date and Wolfgang Köhler at the other. Both men were too great and grand to take issue with. Yet both had the same pallid, ready answer to why things were the way they were—namely, that things were the way they were because the brain is the way it is. Yet they didn't know much about the way the brain was *as related to its effect on psychological matters.* Neither do I. Neither do you. Of course, the most future reader will know much more. But I assume you are reading this today or maybe tomorrow.

This carping point was answered long ago by Köhler, who was always forearmed. Some will say it does not matter, he wrote concerning his particularly brainy views of things, because since you cannot look into the brain you cannot decide who is right. But, he admonishes, that would be an awful misunderstanding, because hypotheses that have concrete content have concrete implications that can be tested. That is true, though complicated (Köhler, 1947).

An aim of this book was to clarify the theoretic basis of the study of thought. While the intention to speak to the basis of the study of thought is obviously a very ambitious one, the work is limited to some very simple tactics. The nontrivial study of thought seems impossible to all very wise people, fruitless to all wise people, very difficult to all very intelligent people, and metaphysically hopeless to everyone else. What was needed is a chimneysweep to chop an open path for the escape of smoke and gases. Therefore, I asserted that there are three parts to thought. Each of these three parts was considered. For each a simplified theoretical basis was described; an algorithm was given for each, and protocols of the use of the algorithms were given.

The term "algorithm" means method, or procedure. Lately the word has been taken up by computer theorists and allied mathematicians. The word is assumed to be a corruption of the name of the man who brought algebra to Europe, whom we met (Chapter 5, p. 75) as not using symbolism. The specific algorithms described, if they are used, are for the use of people; they would have to be drastically transformed for the use of machines, dolphins, honeybees, or geniuses.

Anyone who has wrestled with computer programming knows, to his sorrow, that programs and algorithms do not simplify inquiry. Rather they make the direction of the work *painfully* clear. A computer goes straight through a terribly tedious procedure to come at the end to a result; its glory is that it is *fast*. The writing of a program or an algorithm requires great alertness and patience—everything must be made painfully and haltingly explicit. Following an algorithm also requires patience. As Justus Buchler (1961, p. 86) pointed out, groping is one price a finite creature has to pay in searching according to a method; I add that "repugnant docility" is another.

In a passing observation, Buchler noted (p. 89) that method arises when man comes to recognize his ability to repeat—"to repeat anything at all." It is repetition that is the basis of thought as it occurs naturally, as well as thought when it is exposed and unambiguous, and its cycle of oscillation is brought under some degree of control.

References

Adler, F. H. *Physiology of the eye*. St. Louis: Mosby, 1965.

Adrian, E. D. *The mechanism of nervous action*. Philadelphia: University of Pennsylvania Press, 1959.

Aitken, A. C. The art of mental calculation. *Transactions of The Society of Engineers*, London, December, 1954.

Amster, H. Semantic satiation and generation: Learning? Adaptation? *Psychological Bulletin*, 1964, *62*, 273–286.

Arieti, S. *Interpretation of schizophrenia*. New York: Brunner, 1955.

Barnett, S. A. Book review. *Scientific American*, 1967, *216*, 142.

Bell, E. T. *The development of mathematics*, 2nd ed. New York: McGraw-Hill, 1945.

Békésy, G. von. *Sensory Inhibition*. Princeton, N.J.: Princeton University Press, 1967.

Beveridge, W. I. B. *The art of scientific investigation*, rev. ed. New York: Random House, 1957.

Bragg, L. The art of talking about science. *Science*, 1966, *154*, 1613–1616.

Buchler, J. *The concept of method*. New York: Columbia University Press, 1961.

Burgess, A. *A clockwork orange*. London: Heinemann, 1962.

Crovitz, H. F. The form of logical solutions. *The American Journal of Psychology*, 1967, *80*, 461–462.

Crovitz, H. F., Schiffman, H., and Rees, J. N. Simulation of mental deficiency: The stupid-reader effect. *Psychological Reports*, 1967, *20*, 834.

Davson, H. *The physiology of the eye*, 2nd ed. London: Churchill, 1963.

Duncker, K. (L. S. Lees, trans.). On problem solving. *Psychological Monographs*, 1945, *58* (5, Whole No. 270).

Eiduson, B. T. *Scientists: Their psychological world*. New York: Basic Books, 1962.

Feynman, R. *The character of physical law*. Boston: M.I.T. Press, 1965.

Frank, P. G. *The validation of scientific theories*. New York: Collier, 1961.

154

Galton, F. Psychometric experiments. *Brain*, 1879, 2, 148–162.

Galton, F. *Inquiries into human faculty and its development*. New York: Dutton, 1907.

Gardner, M. *Logic machines, diagrams and Boolean algebra*. New York: Dover, 1968.

Gardner, N. B., and Gardner, B. T. Teaching sign language to a Chimpanzee. *Science*, 1969, *165*, 664–672.

Golann, S. E. Psychological study of creativity. *Psychological Bulletin*, 1963, 60, 548–565.

Graham, E. C. *The basic dictionary of science*. New York: Macmillan, 1965.

Graves, R. *The white goddess*. New York: Vintage, 1958.

Gray, P. H. The analysis of behaviorism: The conscious automaton theory from Spalding to William James. *Journal of the History of the Behavioral Sciences*, 1968, 4, 365–376.

Huxley, T. H. *Method and results*. New York: Appleton-Century-Crofts, 1895.

Hastings, J., Ed. *Encyclopedia of religion and ethics*, vol. IX, 847–855; vol. X, 213–214. New York: Scribner, 1928.

Helmholtz, H. von. *Treatise on physiological optics*. J. P. C. Southall, trans. New York: Dover, 1962.

Holmes, O. W. Sun-painting and sun-sculpture, *Atlantic Monthly*, 1861, *8*, 13–29.

Hull, C. L. Principles of behavior. New York: Appleton-Century-Crofts, 1943.

Hume, D. *Treatise of human nature*, 1739.

James, W. *Principles of psychology*. New York: Holt, Rinehart and Winston, 1890.

Jensen, A. R., and Rohwer, W. D., Jr. Verbal mediation in paired-associate and serial learning. *Journal of Verbal Learning and Verbal Behavior*, 1963, *1*, 346–352.

Jones, E. The nature of genius. *British Medical Journal*, 1956, 2, 257–262.

Josephson, M. *Edison*. New York: McGraw-Hill, 1959.

Kahneman, D., Beatty, J., and Pollack, I. Perceptual deficit during a mental task. *Science*, 1967, *157*, 218–219.

Kedrov, B. M. On the question of scientific creativity. *Soviet Psychology*, Winter 1966–1967, *5*, 16–37.

Klein, M. J. Einstein and some civilized discontents. *Physics Today*, 1965, *18*, 39.

Koestler, A. *The act of creation*. New York: Macmillan, 1964.

Köhler, W. *Gestalt psychology*. New York: Liveright, 1947.

Kogan, Z. *Essentials in problem solving*, 2nd ed. New York: Arco, 1965.

Lecours, A.-R. Serial order in writing—a case of misspelled words in a case of "developmental dysgraphia." *Neuropsychologia*, 1966, *4*, 221–241.

Legge, J., trans. *The I Ching*. New York: Dover, 1963.

Lillie, R. S. Resemblances between the electromotor variations of rhythmically reacting living and non-living systems. *Journal of General Physiology*, 1929, *13*, 1–11.

Lockhead, G. R. A re-evaluation of evidence of one-trial associative learning. *American Journal of Psychology*, 1961, 74, 590–595.

Luchins, A. S. Mechanization in problem-solving: The effect of Einstellung. *Psychological Monographs*, 1942, *54* (Whole No. 248).

Luria, A. R. *The mind of a mnemonist*. New York: Basic Books, 1968.

Mach, E. *The analysis of sensations*. New York: Dover, 1959.

Mandler, J. M., and Mandler, G. *Thinking: From association to Gestalt*. New York: Wiley, 1964.

Max, L. W. An experimental study of the motor theory of consciousness. *Journal of General Psychology*, 1934, *11*, 112–125.

Miller, G. *In* S. S. Stevens, ed., *Handbook of experimental psychology*, New York: Wiley, 1951.

Newell, A., Shaw, J. C., and Simon, H. A. Elements of a theory of human problem solving. *Psychological Review*, 1958, *65*, 151–166.

Norman, D. A. *Memory and attention: An introduction to human information processing*. New York: Wiley, 1969.

Norman, D. A. Memory while shadowing. *Quarterly Journal of Experimental Psychology*, 1969, *21*, 85–93.

Ogden, C. K. *The system of Basic English*. New York: Harcourt, Brace & World, 1934.

Paivio, A. Abstractness, imagery and meaningfulness in paired-associate learning. *Journal of Verbal Learning and Verbal Behavior*. 1965, *4*, 32–38.

Pearson, K. *The life, letters and labours of Francis Galton*. Cambridge: Cambridge University Press, 1914.

Pearson, Karl, *The grammar of science*. London: Dent, 1935.

Peers, E. A. *Ramon Lull, a biography*. London: Society for Promoting Christian Knowledge, 1929.

Poe, E. A. *Tales of mystery and imagination*. New York: Dutton, 1963.

Polya, G. *How to solve it*. New York: Doubleday, 1957.

Polya, G. *Patterns of plausible inference*. Princeton, N. J.: Princeton University Press, 1954.

Reynolds, N. B. Common English please. *Science*, 1967, *158*, 995–996.

Rock, I. The role of repetition in associative learning. *American Journal of Psychology*, 1957, 70, 186–193.

Roe, A. *The making of a scientist*. New York: Dodd, Mead, 1952.

Russell, B. *A history of Western philosophy*. New York: Simon & Schuster, 1945.

Skinner, B. F. *Verbal behavior*. New York: Appleton-Century-Crofts, 1957.

Spalding, D. A. The relation of mind and body. *Nature*, 1874, *9*, 178–179.

Szent-Gyorgyi, A. Lost in the twentieth century. *Annual Review of Biochemistry*, 1963, 32, 1–14.

Teuber, H.-L. Perception. *In Handbook of physiology*, vol. III, Neurophysiology. Washington: American Physiological Society, 1960. Ch. LXV, pp. 1595–1668.

Usher, A. P. *A history of mechanical inventions*, 2nd ed. Boston: Beacon Press, 1954.

Uspenskii, V. A. *Some applications of mechanics to mathematics*. London: Pergamon, 1961.

Vygotsky, L. S. *Thought and language*. New York: Wiley, 1962.

Wallach, M. A., and Kogan, N. *Modes of thinking in young children: A study of the creativity-intelligence distinction*. New York: Holt, Rinehart and Winston, 1965.

Wallas, Graham. The art of thought. London: Cape, 1926.

Waugh, N. Book review. *American Scientist*, 1968, *56*, 326A-327A.

Wheatstone, C. The Bakerian lecture—Contributions to the physiology of vision, Part the Second. *Philosophical Transactions*, 1852.

Woodworth, R. S. *Experimental psychology*. New York: Holt, Rinehart and Winston, 1938.

Yates, F. A. *The art of memory*. Chicago: The University of Chicago Press, 1966.

Index